The *Shema* and John 10

The *Shema* and John 10

The Importance of the *Shema* Framework in Understanding the Oneness Language in John 10

BRURY EKO SAPUTRA

WIPF & STOCK • Eugene, Oregon

THE SHEMA AND JOHN 10
The Importance of the Shema Framework in Understanding the Oneness Language in John 10

Copyright © 2019 Brury Eko Saputra. All rights reserved. Except for brief quotations in critical publications or reviews, no part of this book may be reproduced in any manner without prior written permission from the publisher. Write: Permissions, Wipf and Stock Publishers, 199 W. 8th Ave., Suite 3, Eugene, OR 97401.

Wipf & Stock
An Imprint of Wipf and Stock Publishers
199 W. 8th Ave., Suite 3
Eugene, OR 97401

www.wipfandstock.com

PAPERBACK ISBN: 978-1-5326-7391-7
HARDCOVER ISBN: 978-1-5326-7392-4
EBOOK ISBN: 978-1-5326-7393-1

Manufactured in the U.S.A.   MARCH 19, 2019

For my beloved parent:
Then Bun Sia
Cong Lie Man

Contents

Preface | ix
Acknowledgments | xi
Introduction | xiii

1. The *Shema* and the Oneness Language in the Gospel of John | 1
2. The *Shema* as the Framework | 30
3. The *Shema* and John 10 (1) | 48
4. The *Shema* and John 10 (2) | 55
5. Conclusion | 80

Bibliography | 85

Preface

I AM ALWAYS FASCINATED with the concept of God. During my initial theological training at Aletheia Theological Seminary (Sekolah Tinggi Teologi Aletheia), in Lawang, Malang (Indonesia), I explored the concept of God in the thought of German philosopher Georg Wilhelm Friedrich Hegel as my final project. After that, I had the opportunity to further my theological training at Trinity Theological College in Singapore. I used the time I had there to explore again the concept of God, not only philosophically but also biblically. During the exploration, I came to one particular interest, that is the idea of the oneness of God in the New Testament and early Christianity. I thus wrote a thesis on the oneness language of the Gospel of John in connection with the Jewish understanding of the oneness of God (the *Shema*). This book is an upgraded version of my work in the thesis.

The idea of writing this book first came to me during my study at Trinity Theological College. I was surprised by the fact that there were not many books written on the oneness language of John's Gospel, let alone on the *Shema* as an interpretative key. Thus, I explored the possibility of the *Shema* having a sort of connection with the oneness language of John's Gospel. Having made a preliminary exploration, I asked myself a question: "Is it possible to construct a framework using the *Shema* to read the oneness language of John's Gospel?" Using John 10 as a "sample," this book is an attempt towards answering that question. In the end, with the awareness that this book has many weaknesses, I hope that this book will contribute to the field, help theological students, and be useful to pastors.

Acknowledgments

As previously mentioned in the preface, large materials of this book originate from my revised master thesis materials done at Trinity Theological College, Singapore. That said, this book would not be existed without my theological training there. I, therefore, am indebted to the College and especially to my supervisor, Professor Tan Kim Huat. I also want to thank Professor Simon Chan of Trinity Theological College for the encouragement, discussion, and coffee time. My gratitude goes also for the support from my colleagues and students at Aletheia Theological Seminary, including the coffee time I had with Dr. Sia Kok Sin, Dr. Kornelius A. Setiawan, Dr. Amos Winarto, and Rev. Linus Baito. Last but not least, I owe my utmost thanks to my family, Su Fang and Alistair Alden Saputra. Their support during the finishing of the manuscript was invaluable.

Introduction

SINCE THE FIRST CENTURY, the Gospel of John has been deemed special by the church. The early church fathers believed that the Gospel of John was different from other Gospels (known as the Synoptic today). It is called the spiritual gospel for its unique presentation of Jesus. In this book, I want to confirm that its uniqueness can also be found in its use of the oneness language. In doing so, this book will be structured as follows: chapter 1 of the book will survey the previous studies on the oneness motif in the Gospel of John. There are four works surveyed in this chapter. The first is a book by Mark L. Appold. In his book, Appold argues that the oneness language of the Gospel of John has to be understood against its Hellenistic background. What is intriguing about his study is his way of explaining (or more precisely, clarifying) the nature of the oneness language in the Gospel of John as the oneness of revelation and the oneness of relationship. The present book is benefiting from his explanation. The second is an unpublished dissertation by Far-Dung Tong. In his dissertation, Tong offers an interesting approach to reading the oneness language of the Gospel. He argues that the oneness language has anything to do with Judaism of the period. The present book agrees with his conclusion, but finds no specific reference to the Judaism he mentioned in his work.

The third work is a book by Andrew J. Byers. Different from the two works previously mentioned above, this book argues not only that Judaism is important for understanding the oneness language of the Gospel, but also points specifically to the *Shema*

Introduction

as an interpretative key. The primary focus of this book is on the ecclesiology as an integral element of John's theology and Christology. Byers presents a case that by reading the oneness language in light of the *Shema*, John's ecclesiology can be understood in the *theosis* (deification) language. I agree and have benefited from this study, but also think an investigation of the oneness language of the Gospel should take the historical context into consideration. The fourth study is an unpublished dissertation by Lori Ann Robinson Baron. Just like Byers, Baron argues that the *Shema* heavily influences the oneness language of John's Gospel. But unlike Byers, Baron demonstrates that the historical context—that is, the two-level drama proposed by Louis Martyn—plays an important role in understanding the oneness language. I agree with Baron's assertion that the *Shema* and the historical context are important, but am not convinced by Martyn's proposal.

Chapter 2 is an attempt to construct a framework—called the *Shema* Framework—to read the oneness language found in John 10. This chapter argues that there are three important aspects of the *Shema*, for which a framework can be constructed. Those aspects are: 1) The theological aspect which states the oneness of God as the most important element of the *Shema*; 2) The ecclesiological aspect which determines the identity of God's people as can also be found in the use of the *Shema* in the Second Temple period; and 3) The eschatological aspect which points to the one future of the people of God.

Chapter 3 is dedicated to exploring the echoes of the *Shema* in John 10. In doing so, this chapter will try to investigate the presence of the *Shema* elements such as the oneness, love, hearing, and deliverance motifs. Surprisingly, John 10 has utilized all those motifs around Jesus and His people. In chapter 4, I will try to apply the framework proposed in chapter 2 into the findings of chapter 3. The present book will conclude with chapter 5 in which I will summarize the result of the reading in chapter 4. In the end, I hope that this small book will contribute to the study of the oneness language of the Gospel of John.

I

The *Shema* and the Oneness Language in the Gospel of John

IT IS EVIDENT, EVEN from the second century, that the Gospel of John is full of profound theological concepts. However, two thousand years since then, not all of them have been fully explored. One of them is the oneness motif found in the Gospel. Currently, there are (possibly only) four extensive studies on the subject.

The Oneness Motif in the Fourth Gospel

The first study is originally a dissertation submitted to the University of Tübingen by Mark L. Appold.[1] This study aims to be "an extensive study devoted specifically to the theme of oneness as a basic Johannine motif"[2] In doing so, it tries to demonstrate the centrality of the oneness motif in the Fourth Gospel. It begins with assessing the weaknesses of previous studies in the field. Previous studies, according to Appold, tend to approach the oneness motif in the Fourth Gospel as an expression of mysticism, like love (Dodd), will (Thüsing), organic oneness (Barret), and morality

1. Appold, *The Oneness*.
2. Appold, *The Oneness*, 13

(Bauer).³ However, those claims need to be reexamined.⁴ The arguments of this study can be summarized as follows:

The Oneness of Relationship-Revelation

Appold demonstrates how skillfully he handles the text through his overview of the use of the word one (εἷς) in the Gospel.⁵ He argues that the word εἷς is used in connection with the notion of relationship and revelation.⁶ The former refers to the relationship of Jesus and the Father, which directly connects with the latter, the revelation of their identity as the Son and the Father.⁷ That relationship becomes a foundation for the oneness of the believers.⁸ In other words, the oneness in the Fourth Gospel has to be understood as the oneness of relationship and revelation. The notion of the oneness of relationship is further demonstrated by examining the reciprocity statements (e.g., through the use of the following verbs: πέμπω, ἐργάζομαι, μαρτυρέω, δοξάζω, ἀγαπάω).⁹ Appold argues that the reciprocity statements' "function is distinctively unique" so as to indicate Jesus' relationship to the Father and his own.¹⁰ In those statements, Jesus is portrayed as one with the Father, (e.g., John 7:29; 14:7, 9; 10:38¹¹ and his own.¹² Through his presence and

---

3. Appold, *The Oneness*, 14–6
4. Appold, *The Oneness*, 17
5. Appold, *The Oneness*, 11–2
6. Appold concludes that the word εἷς is oriented in 1) Its Christological use as a revelatory indicator expressing the unique relation of Jesus to the Father. 2) Its soteriological significance in indicating that the possibility of faith exists only in response to and in oneness with the heavenly reality manifested in the works of Father and Son. 3) Its ecclesiological significance in describing the solidary character of the chosen one. See Appold, *The Oneness*, 12–3.
7. Appold, *The Oneness*, 27–28, 32–33
8. Appold, *The Oneness*, 34, 41, 45–46
9. Appold, *The Oneness*, 18–33
10. Appold, *The Oneness*, 18, 34
11. Appold, *The Oneness*, 18–9
12. Appold, *The Oneness*, 34–6

The Shema and the Oneness Language in the Gospel of John

works, Jesus reveals the Father, who is one with him, to the world.[13] This constitutes the notion of the oneness of revelation.[14]

Those findings, according to Appold, correspond with other aspects of the Gospel. They correspond with the use of the Christological titles in the Fourth Gospel. There are six explicit titles (and some other implicit ones); these are the Son of Man, Son of God, Son, Christ, Prophet, and King. All of the titles, including the ἐγώ εἰμι statements,[15] are evidently closely connected to the oneness motif in the Fourth Gospel.[16] More precisely, the titles are placed in the context of the oneness of Jesus and the Father. Furthermore, the oneness of revelation also corresponds with the passion narrative of the Fourth Gospel. The passion account is colored with the revelation of the identity of Jesus. As an example, the story of Lazarus emphasizes not only the miracle performed by Jesus, but the revelation of Jesus' identity to his disciples.[17]

Gnosticism and the Oneness Motif of the Fourth Gospel

In his study, Appold uses source-criticism developed by Bultmann as his methodology (chapter 6). Although Bultmann's approach has recently been challenged by many, Appold finds that the approach is still useful for Johannine studies. One contribution of Bultmann's approach to Johannine studies is that he has strenuously argued for the use of Gnostic sources in the Fourth Gospel.[18] Bultmann's work becomes a foundation for Appold's investigation on the Fourth Gospel, as can be seen primarily from chapters 7 to 9. In those chapters, Appold examines three oneness passages: the departing prayer of Jesus (John 17), Caiaphas's prophetic statement (John 11:47–53), and the shepherd discourse (John 10). He

13. Appold, *The Oneness*, 34
14. Appold, *The Oneness*, 34–47
15. Appold, *The Oneness*, 81
16. Appold, *The Oneness*, 53, 58, 63, 66, 74, 77
17. Appold, *The Oneness*, 124
18. Appold, *The Oneness*, 155

The Shema and John 10

applies the same pattern in approaching those three passages, e.g., structural considerations, stylistic factors and religio-historical comparisons. Structural considerations demonstrate, according to Appold, the peculiarity of the passages of the Fourth Gospel. Stylistic factors confirm that the passages are integral parts of the gospel. Finally, the religio-historical comparisons show that the passages are rooted in Gnosticism.

In the larger context, Appold insists, the prayer of Jesus in John 17 is comparable to Mandaean Gnosis.[19] He contends that the concept of the oneness of the community in John 17 is rooted in the concept of *Laufa* or communion.[20] In Mandean Gnosis, the *Laufa* is an essential character of the heavenly reality which bounds the revealer and the believers in unity.[21] In addition, the *Laufa* is also an important character in the earthly reflection of the heavenly reality.[22] The importance is captured in a ritual called the *Kusta* handshake which symbolizes both faithfulness and truthfulness of the members of the community.[23] In other words, each member is "bound together in a communion that is a projection of the communion of the transcendent world."[24] The same can be said about the religious background of John 11:52—the gathering of the children of God.[25] Although, there are many similarities in vocabulary and context between the Gospel and the Old Testament, it seems to be implausible for the evangelist to use them as the background.[26] Appold rather argues that the concept of gathering in the Gospel is rooted in Gnosticism (e.g., the *Laufa* and *Kusta* traditions).[27] Not only similar expressions are found between the Gospel and Gnostic sources, but they also have a similar

19. Appold, *The Oneness*, 186–92
20. Appold, *The Oneness*, 186
21. Appold, *The Oneness*, 187
22. Appold, *The Oneness*, 189
23. Appold, *The Oneness*, 189
24. Appold, *The Oneness*, 189
25. Appold, *The Oneness*, 243
26. Appold, *The Oneness*, 243
27. Appold, *The Oneness*, 244

The Shema and the Oneness Language in the Gospel of John

soteriological goal.[28] As for John 10, Appold insists that "although the Old Testament shepherd tradition shows undeniable lines of correspondence with the shepherd motif in chapter 10, it is nevertheless not broad enough to parallel the characteristically new accents introduced in that chapter."[29] The new accents mentioned are similar to "expressions peculiar to distinctly Gnostic traditions."[30]

The Oneness and the Theology of the Fourth Gospel

In the last chapter, Appold presents the theological implications of his study. According to him, "the oneness motif appears as a theological abbreviation for the evangelist's deepest concern."[31] Interestingly, the oneness as a theological abbreviation is found nowhere in other New Testament writings.[32] There are three theological implications that need to be noted here. First, the ecclesiology of the Fourth Gospel is based on its Christology.[33] For John, according to Appold, the church is not a continuation of Old Testament Israel.[34] Membership in the church is determined by one's response to the oneness of the Father and Jesus.[35] Those who are integrated with the oneness of the Father and Jesus are bound together in intimacy and closeness.[36] The intimacy and closeness are an earthly projection of the heavenly reality in John's community.[37]

Secondly, the soteriological aspect of the oneness motif is closely connected with ecclesiology.[38] Here, the gathering of the children of God (ecclesiology) is a medium to bring salvation

28. Appold, *The Oneness*, 244
29. Appold, *The Oneness*, 260
30. Appold, *The Oneness*, 260
31. Appold, *The Oneness*, 262
32. Appold, *The Oneness*, 289–94
33. Appold, *The Oneness*, 262–72
34. Appold, *The Oneness*, 263
35. Appold, *The Oneness*, 265
36. Appold, *The Oneness*, 265–6, 286–7
37. Appold, *The Oneness*, 268–9
38. Appold, *The Oneness*, 272–9

(soteriology). The process of the gathering into one is done by Jesus through his death—of which he is exalted and glorified (John 11:52).[39] It means that Jesus' death functions as the revelation of himself and the Father to all people. In this case, the salvation in John is neither for the Jews nor gentiles, but to all who believe—the children of God.[40] Technically, John's ecclesiology is not "that of harmony, or of an organism, or of the body of Christ, but of the faith event in which one's relation to the heavenly reality demonstrated in Jesus' oneness with the Father establishes an equivalent relation among the believers."[41]

The third implication concerns the relationship of the oneness motif with John's Christology.[42] Appold argues that the oneness motif of the Fourth Gospel underlines the oneness of the Father and Jesus—Jesus is in the Father (John 17:21) and conversely that the Father is in Jesus (John 11:21, 23).[43] This oneness is demonstrated by the works (including the sending of the Son) performed by Jesus during his earthly life.[44] This is not to say that Jesus acquires or achieves the oneness with God, but rather his deeds reveal his oneness with God.[45] Consequently, "Jesus' oneness with the Father must be spoken of in both relational and revelational terms."[46] In other words, the oneness in the Fourth Gospel can be said as an abbreviation of the evangelist's Christology.

Comments on Appold's Approach

Appold has successfully identified the weaknesses of previous studies in this field. According to him, a framework such as moral or metaphysical oneness is actually inadequate for understanding

39. Cf. Appold, *The Oneness*, 274
40. Appold, *The Oneness*, 278
41. Appold, *The Oneness*, 279
42. Appold, *The Oneness*, 280–9
43. Appold, *The Oneness*, 282
44. Appold, *The Oneness*, 283
45. Appold, *The Oneness*, 282
46. Appold, *The Oneness*, 283

the oneness motif in the Fourth Gospel. On the contrary, he suggests that the oneness in the Fourth Gospel has to be seen in connection with the idea of relationship and revelation. The oneness of relationship means the oneness that shows the unique relationship between Jesus and the Father. In this relationship, Jesus and the Father are presented as equal and personal. The oneness of revelation, on the other hand, means that the oneness language used in the Fourth Gospel functions as a medium to reveal God the Father to the world. Interestingly, such language is exclusively applied to Jesus, referring to his coming, works, and even death. It means the Father is revealed to the world through Jesus' presence. That is "theology proper" in the Fourth Gospel. Furthermore, to understand the oneness motif in the Fourth Gospel as the oneness of revelation, readers of the Fourth Gospel are basically driven to understand its Christology, soteriology, and ecclesiology as intended by the Gospel's author. The Christological aspect of the oneness language can be seen in the presentation of Jesus as the representative of the Father. The soteriological aspect can be understood in the response of the people to God's revelation in Jesus. The ecclesiological aspect can be perceived in the relationship of Jesus and the Father as being mirrored in the relationship of Jesus with the people (John 10; 17).

Appold makes a strong case when he says that the oneness motif in the Gospel of John has to be understood as the oneness of relationship and revelation. However, he is not convincing when he deals with the source, tradition and context of the oneness motif in the Gospel of John. He confidently conjectures that the nature of the relational and revelational oneness must have come from Gnostic sources. There are some points worth considering regarding this assumption. The first to note is the form/source criticism he inherited from Bultmann and Käsemann. The methodology has been challenged and considered as inadequate in dealing with Gospel writings by many scholars. Richard Bauckham comprehensively summarizes the arguments demonstrating its weaknesses.[47] Secondly, the connection between the Fourth

---

47. Bauckham, *Jesus and the Eyewitnesses*, 246–8. There are nine points

Gospel and Gnosticism is questionable. C.H. Dodd in his *The Interpretation of the Fourth Gospel* shows that the conjecture about Gnostic influences upon the Fourth Gospel is no longer tenable. It is simply because Gnostic sources are later than the Fourth Gospel.[48] From a different angle, Dodd's conclusion is supported by a recently published book, *The Johannine Corpus in the Early Church*, by Charles E. Hill. Hill challenges a common conjecture that the Fourth Gospel was accepted relatively late by the orthodox as compared to some Gnostic groups; with the putative reason being that the Fourth Gospel was loaded with Gnosticism.[49] He contends that there is evidence to show the use of the Fourth Gospel by the early (Orthodox) Church even before 150 CE.[50] The early acceptance of the Fourth Gospel, in many forms (e.g., liturgy), by the early church shows that Fourth Gospel's theology (including its oneness motif) was no stranger to the early church.

Thirdly, the traditions influencing the Gospel of John have to be differentiated into cultural and theological influences. In this regard, John D. Turner's article, "the History of Religious

---

provided by Bauckham in order to show the weaknesses of source/form criticism. 1) There is no reason why the traditions should not have existed from the beginning in modified or mixed forms. 2) There is no strict correlation between a form and a *Sitz im Leben*. 3) The exaggerated assumption of homeostasis is used in form criticism. 4) There is no laws of traditions operating consistently throughout the gospel traditions. 5) The assumption of comparability with folklore can be questioned at several points. 6) Folklorists themselves have abandoned the 'romantic' idea of the folk as collectively the creator of folk traditions in favor of recognizing the roles of authoritative individuals in interaction with the community. 7) The form critics worked with a preconceived notion of the development of early Christianity 8) The notion that the gospel traditions were transmitted purely orally for several decades was assumed by the form critics rather than demonstrated. 9) The use of a literary model to determine the oral traditions is inadequate.

48. Cf. Dodd, *The Interpretation*, 98; Barrett, *The Gospel of John*, 65. For the pre-Gnosticism or proto-Gnosticism influence on John's Gospel, see Barret, "John and Judaism," 401–17.

49. It is evident that the Fourth Gospel was used by Gnostic exegetes since the early of second century. However, it does not necessarily mean that the Fourth Gospel was rooted in Gnosticism nor refuted by the early church.

50. Hill, *The Johannine Corpus*, 360–446.

The Shema *and the Oneness Language in the Gospel of John*

Background of John 10," is worth noting. He claims on the one hand, that the image of the Shepherd in John 10 has a strong connection with the Old Testament, especially Num 27.17 and Ezek 34.[51] On the other, he is also surprised that there are extraordinary parallels between the Johannine Shepherd and the god Hermes (and other Hellenistic traditions).[52] He then concludes that a close reading of the Fourth Gospel reveals that the Hellenistic traditions influenced the Gospel of John culturally, but it is the Jewish traditions that influenced it theologically.[53] Thus, it is right to conclude as Barrett does, "it (Gnosticism/Hellenism) gives form to the language; it (Gnosticism/Hellenism) does not create the thought behind it (the language of the Gospel)."[54] Fourthly, the oneness motif in the Gospel of John is not isolated from the rest of the New Testament writings. There are many passages that mention the relational-revelational oneness theme. 1) It appears in the blessing formula of Paul's Epistles (e.g., 2 Cor 1.2–4; 13.14; Rom 1.7).[55] The blessing formula in these passages shows not merely the relationship of Jesus with the Father (and the Spirit), but also Jesus' relationship with the believers. 2 Corinthians is a good example of that. It can be said that 2 Corinthians uses the blessing formula as an inclusion. It appears in 2 Cor 1:2–4 and 2 Cor 13:14. The former passage reveals that Jesus is the revelation of God. Jesus' relationship with the Father is also clearly presented in a way that comforts the believers (2 Cor 1:4–6). In 2 Cor 13:14, the same picture is presented, where Jesus and the Father are presented as the one who gives grace and mercy to the community of believers. That passage is actually comparable to John 17, where Jesus prays for the believers. 2) The oneness of relation-revelation is also mentioned in the

---

51. Turner, "The History," 49–50. Cf. Bultmann, *The Gospel of John*, 384.

52. Turner, "The History," 51.

53. Dodd, *The Interpretation*, 98; Bultmann, *The Gospel of John*, 384; cf. Hoskyns, *The Fourth Gospel*; Schnackenburg, *The Gospel*; Brown, *The Gospel*; Carson, *The Gospel*; Barrett, *The Gospel*.

54. Barret, "John and Judaism," 405.

55. It is also comparable to salutations in Paul's letters. Cf. Howell, "God-Christ Interchange in Paul," 468–70.

The Shema and John 10

polemical passages in the New Testament (e.g., 1 Cor 8; 12; Phil 2:5–11). 1 Cor 8:6 is arguably the most famous monotheistic statement in a polemical context. However, Appold insists that the passage does not show the relational-revelational motif. In this case, it is important to compare 1 Cor 8 with John 10. Notably, the two are set in polemical contexts: 1 Cor 8 concerns food offering, while John 10 Jesus' identity. Furthermore, 1 Cor 8:3 and John 10:4, 14 show that the "knowing" motif is strongly connected with the oneness motif. In addition, the theme of Jesus' death is also common in both texts (1 Cor 8:11, John 10:15, 17). The point of contact, in terms of the oneness motif, of 1 Cor 8 and John 10, can also be seen in verse 6 of the former, where Paul proclaims the oneness of God and Jesus—"there is only one God and one Lord." In this case, Paul is actually arguing that the relationship of Jesus and God is intimate as they are both the sole creator of all things. In other words, God's creative power is revealed through and in the person of Jesus. Consequently, this oneness (relational-revelational) has become a foundation for the oneness of the community (cf. 1 Cor 12).[56] 3) The relational-revelational oneness can also be found in eschatological passages (e.g., 1 Cor 15; 1 Tess 3; 4; Rev 4–5) and the baptism formula (Matt 28:19). Although the term "one" is missing in those texts, the idea is implied by the presentation of the togetherness of Jesus and the Father (see 1 Cor 15). In the case of the baptism formula, the oneness is seen not only through the togetherness, but also the inseparable relationship, which includes the sharing of power and authority (see Matt 28:19–20).

Gathering into One

This study is an unpublished dissertation written by Far-Dung Tong in 1983.[57] He begins with analyzing modern approaches to the study of the oneness motif of the Fourth Gospel. According to him, modern scholarship in this field has relied too much on

---

56. Wright, *The Climax*, 132–35.
57. Tong, "Gathering into One"

The Shema and the Oneness Language in the Gospel of John

either Judaism or the Hellenistic background in order to understand the oneness motif in the Gospel of John.[58] On the contrary, he proposes to use both Judaism and the Hellenistic background for the study.[59] He argues that John 10:16 is a central passage for understanding the oneness motif in the Gospel of John. It also sets the foundation for understanding John 17. John 10:16 shows that the oneness is closely connected with John's Christology and Ecclesiology. It means the oneness of God's people is determined by their relationship with the Shepherd.[60] The arguments of this work can be summarized in the following sections:

Soteriology as an Interpretative Key

In his work, Tong stresses the importance of soteriology for understanding the oneness motif (see chapters 4–5).[61] Its importance can be seen in the life-giving action performed by the one shepherd and the election of his own.[62] Soteriology in Jesus' death is not seen as a vicarious act, but a lifting-up-act, in which the glory of Christ is shown to the world.[63] The election as part of John's soteriological act shows that the children of God are gathered into one as Jesus and the Father are one.[64] In other words, through the election, other aspects of the oneness are revealed. The importance of soteriology can further be seen in the passages like John 11:47–53; 12:24; 18:19. In John 18:19, it is evident that "those who receive eternal life are those given by the Father, and drawn by the Son,"[65] which indicates the importance of soteriology for understanding

---

58. Tong, "Gathering into One," 10–36
59. Tong, "Gathering into One," 36–7
60. Tong, "Gathering into One," 46–50
61. Tong, "Gathering into One," 48–53
62. Tong, "Gathering into One," 48
63. Tong, "Gathering into One," 104–6
64. Tong, "Gathering into One," 107–10
65. Tong, "Gathering into One," 79

the oneness motif in the Fourth Gospel. In short, the motif of the oneness language of the Fourth Gospel is soteriological.[66]

The Oneness and the Gathering

Tong concludes that the concept of the gathering into one represents the oneness motif of the Fourth Gospel. It has its background in both the Old Testament and Gnosticism.[67] The Old Testament concept of the gathering into one can be traced back to Zion theology—God will gather his own in Zion.[68] However, the gathering in Gnosticism can be understood as an act of gathering the scattered lights or seeds from the darkness.[69] These two traditions contribute to the soteriological aspect of the oneness motif in the Fourth Gospel (as mentioned earlier), i.e., salvation is known through and marked by the gathering of God's people. The people must be gathered into one for their God is one.[70] In other words, the gathering into one does not refer to the church as an institution, but as the representative of the oneness of the Father and Son/heavenly reality.[71] In summary, the gathering into one is a presentation of the oneness motif in the Fourth Gospel in which the oneness of Jesus with the Father and with his own is depicted.

Comments on Tong's Approach

In his study, Tong has pointed out the weaknesses of some modern approaches to the study of the oneness motif in the Fourth Gospel. He is right when he insists that besides Hellenistic influences, it is evident that the Fourth Gospel has a Jewish background. He suggests that both the Jewish and Hellenistic influences need to be

66. Tong, "Gathering into One," 71–2
67. Tong, "Gathering into One," 117
68. Tong, "Gathering into One," 19–28
69. Tong, "Gathering into One," 11–8
70. Tong, "Gathering into One," 57–9
71. Tong, "Gathering into One," 61–5

considered in understanding the oneness language of the Fourth Gospel. By Jewish influences he means the Old Testament. However, the Hellenistic influences he mentions refers to Gnosticism. The two, if brought together, will indicate the intention of the fourth evangelist in using the oneness language. In addition, his proposal about the gathering is well executed. It provides a fresh understanding on how to connect the oneness motif with the Zion tradition. However, there are some problems that need to be highlighted.

First, Tong does not clearly define what kind of influences John's Gospel has received from both the Old Testament and Gnosticism. As mentioned earlier, many scholars suggest that the Hellenistic or Gnosticism influences are cultural in nature, whereas the Old Testament influences are theological. Secondly, although he has successfully discussed the importance of the Old Testament for understanding the oneness motif in the Fourth Gospel, he does not consider the importance of Second Temple Judaism and the destruction of the Temple, both could be plausible candidates for influencing and shaping the Fourth Gospel. Thirdly, he does not explain in what sense soteriology can be used as the interpretative key in understanding the oneness motif. To be sure, the gathering into one (ecclesiology) has a close connection with soteriology as seen in the Zion tradition—the one God delivers and gathers His people into one. That there is an ecclesiological aspect to the oneness is understandable, but it does not in itself explain the oneness of Jesus and the Father.

Ecclesiology and Theosis in the Gospel of John

The book is originally a dissertation submitted to Durham University in 2014 by Andrew J. Byers. The book focuses on the ecclesiology of the Gospel of John. The primary claims of the book are:

> 1) Ecclesiology is not a secondary or ancillary theme for John but one that appears just as prominently in the Prologue as Christology and wields normative force over the entire Gospel; 2) the concept of oneness, universally

recognized as a critical motif for Johannine ecclesiology, is grounded in the theological oneness of the *Shema* ("YHWH is one"—Deut. 6:4); and 3) the Gospel portrays the human community of believers undergoing such a striking transformation for the sake of divine participation that recourse to the patristic language of "theosis" is both warranted and exegetically promising."[72]

Using the concept of "theosis" mentioned above, Byers understands the Gospel of John as a "deification narrative," meaning "to be 'one' with the Christologically reconceived divine identity refers to something more profound than a state of ecumenical harmony, internal social unity, or unity in function or will with God."[73]

After surveying what he groups as four approaches in the Johannine Ecclesiology, Byers aligns his approach with "the diverse range of exegetical strategies available in narrative criticism."[74] In using such an approach, he tries to offer a more comprehensive treatment of the Johannine Ecclesiology.[75] The comprehensive treatment he mentioned is demonstrated by structuring the book into three major parts in which the first two of them will be surveyed in the following section; the first part deals with the Prologue of the Gospel while the second "offers a narrative re-reading of the Johannine conceptuality of 'one'"[76] His arguments in those two parts can be summarized as follows:

The Prologue of the Gospel

In part one of the book Byers argues that the presentation of a divine dyad—the relational inter-dynamics of God and the *Logos*—is a foundational for Johannine ecclesiology.[77] This relationship signifies the plurality within the unity of God and the *Logos*. In other

72. Byers, *Ecclesiology and Theosis*, 3
73. Byers, *Ecclesiology and Theosis*, 3
74. Byers, *Ecclesiology and Theosis*, 19
75. Byers, *Ecclesiology and Theosis*, 20
76. Byers, *Ecclesiology and Theosis*, 23
77. Byers, *Ecclesiology and Theosis*, 30

words, although God is perceived as being one with the *Logos* in the Prologue, those two are distinct entities. This interpretation of God is made possible through the reconceptualization of the identity of God as the divine community.[78] Interestingly, as noted by Byers himself, this reconceptualization does not mean that the fourth evangelist is creating a new religion around a new god.[79] Using the term "divine identity," coined by Bauckham, Byers believes that the inclusion of the *Logos* (Jesus) into the divine identity of YHWH makes this divine community consistently understood within the Jewish theological tradition.[80]

Byers asserts that the relationship between God and the *Logos* is later explained by the fourth evangelist using the filial language.[81] In John 1:14 and 1:18, the phrase μονογηνής θεός is applied to Jesus in order to show the divine plurality and divine unity in the filial term; meaning that "Jesus and the Father are understood as sharing the divine identity (as indicated by the latter term in the phrase, θεός, which denotes unity) while existing in an interrelation in which they are distinguishable figures (μονογηνής, denoting plurality)."[82] Byers later explains that the phrase does not indicate nor mean that Jesus is "subsumed within or absorbed into God that his uniquely identifiable existence dissolves into some sort of divine admixture."[83] He later uses the term "disambiguation" to distinguish the Father and *Logos*.[84]

Byers argues that this divine community is the foundation for the Gospel's ecclesiology throughout the Gospel (see his chapter 5). He sees there is a "staircase parallelism" between John 1:1 and 1:3–4.[85] The significance of this parallelism is:

---

78. Byers, *Ecclesiology and Theosis*, 30–1
79. Byers, *Ecclesiology and Theosis*, 33
80. Byers, *Ecclesiology and Theosis*, 30–1
81. Byers, *Ecclesiology and Theosis*, 50–1
82. Byers, *Ecclesiology and Theosis*, 34–6
83. Byers, *Ecclesiology and Theosis*, 36
84. Byers, *Ecclesiology and Theosis*, 50–2
85. Byers, *Ecclesiology and Theosis*, 38

> Just as the Logos (Christology) is eventually correlated to God (theology) in John 1:1, that which is brought into being in John 1:3b is said to be in the Logos (ἐν αὐτῷ) then correlated in some capacity to Life and Light, terms that become emphatically Christological throughout the Johannine Prologue. In linking together key terms, the literary device of concatenation also binds together key themes: Christology is linked to theology in John 1:1; anthropology is linked to Christology in John 1:3b-4.[86]

This pattern, which generally includes humanity (anthropology) into the divine community extends specifically to the inclusion of the people of God (ecclesiology).[87] Consistently, this process of inclusion makes use of the filial language of Jesus as the Son (μονογενής) and God the Father (πατήρ) to the people of God as the children (τέκνα θεοῦ) with God the Father (πατήρ).[88] Such a reading, interestingly, was known and well attested by Patristic interpreters and gradually acknowledged by modern interpreters.[89] In short, as stated by Byers himself, "ecclesiology is a Christological reconfiguring of the social identity of God's people."[90]

The Oneness Narrative Development

In part two, Byers proposes a "new reading"[91] on the oneness language of the Gospel. He believes that the oneness language found in the Gospel is "indebted to the Jewish profession of divine oneness in the *Shema*."[92] It was primarily because of the pervasiveness of the *Shema* in the early Jewish Religious life.[93] Strikingly, he argues,

---

86. Byers, *Ecclesiology and Theosis*, 39
87. Cf. Byers, *Ecclesiology and Theosis*, 48-9, 53, 202
88. Byers, *Ecclesiology and Theosis*, 54-5
89. Byers, *Ecclesiology and Theosis*, 65-71
90. Byers, *Ecclesiology and Theosis*, 44
91. The impetus was firstly triggered by Barret in 1947; see Byers, *Ecclesiology and Theosis*, 109.
92. Byers, *Ecclesiology and Theosis*, 23
93. Byers, *Ecclesiology and Theosis*, 110-6

The Shema and the Oneness Language in the Gospel of John

the oneness language of the Gospel bears the same characteristic as the filial language in the Prologue, noting "just as the divine family is a community that is open to human membership, John's oneness motif is 'open' and 'social.'"[94]

There are several passages of the Gospel studied by Byers in regards to the oneness language and its connection with the *Shema*. Those passages are John 8–11 and John 17. Those passages, according to Byers, were closely related to Deut 6:4; Ezek 34 and 37. John 8:41 (ἕνα πατέρα ἔχομεν τὸν θεόν), Byers argues, echoed the theological oneness of the *Shema* from Deut 6:4–5 (cf. The similarity with Mal 2:10) in which the Jews were referring to the one God as their father in order to restate the social identity they had.[95] The argument is supported by the occurrence of the love motif stated by Jesus in John 8:42.[96] The oneness language appears again in John 10:16 (μία ποίμνη, εἷς ποιμήν) but with a new dimension, drawn from a different set of scriptural texts (Ezek 34 and 37), which stresses the messianic and national oneness instead of the theological one.[97]

The next appearance of the oneness language observed by Byers is found in John 10:30 (ἐγὼ καὶ ὁ πατὴρ ἕν ἐσμεν). The distinctive feature of the oneness language found in this verse is the use of the neuter ἕν instead of the masculine εἷς to include Jesus into the "divine identity" of the one God.[98] Thus, the feature shows that the "oneness is becoming increasingly open and social" over the course of the narrative development of the Gospel.[99] The final instance of the oneness language of John 8–11 is found in 11:47–53. These verses, according to Byers, combine the "ecclesial and Christological oneness drawn from Ezek 34 and 37."[100] The combination is seen through the gathering of the scattered people

---

94. Byers, *Ecclesiology and Theosis*, 105
95. Byers, *Ecclesiology and Theosis*, 131, 134
96. Byers, *Ecclesiology and Theosis*, 131
97. Byers, *Ecclesiology and Theosis*, 134–5
98. Byers, *Ecclesiology and Theosis*, 137, 140
99. Byers, *Ecclesiology and Theosis*, 137
100. Byers, *Ecclesiology and Theosis*, 140.

The Shema and John 10

motif (ecclesiology) by (means of) the death of the one (promised Davidic) Shepherd (Christology; 11:52; cf. 10:11).[101]

Having examined the oneness language found in John 8–11, Byers turns to chapter 17 of the Gospel. In his opinion, contrary to some modern interpretations, the oneness language of John 17 is an extension of the oneness echoed the *Shema* found in John 8–11.[102] The connection can firstly be seen in the priestly function of offering consecration performed by Jesus in John 17:17–19 (cf. 10:36).[103] Secondly, the connection can be identified through the use of "the concept of other sheep" in John 10:16; 11:52; and 17:20.[104] Seeing these connections, Byers confidently concludes that "these connecting threads between John 17 and John 10–11 affirm that oneness in Jesus' prayer must be read in light of previous oneness formulae."[105] By way of summary, Byers says that "to be 'one' in Johannine perspective is to be (re)gathered into the divine community of the Father (Israel's 'one' God) and Jesus (the 'one' messianic king)."[106]

Comments on Byers's Approach

Different from previous works mentioned above, Byers's work proposes a fresh reading of the oneness language of the Gospel; that the oneness language has to be read through the lens of the *Shema*. I agree with Byers that the ecclesiology of the Gospel cannot be separated from its theology which is heavily influenced by the oneness language of the *Shema*. Furthermore, I also am benefiting from his study, especially his reading of the relation between the *Shema* and ecclesiology of the Gospel.

---

101. Byers, *Ecclesiology and Theosis*, 141.
102. Byers, *Ecclesiology and Theosis*, 144–6
103. Byers, *Ecclesiology and Theosis*, 145
104. Byers, *Ecclesiology and Theosis*, 145–6
105. Byers, *Ecclesiology and Theosis*, 146
106. Byers, *Ecclesiology and Theosis*, 146

The Shema *and the Oneness Language in the Gospel of John*

Having said that, however, my book will differ from his in two ways. Firstly, while Byers approaches the Gospel and its oneness language using "the diverse range of exegetical strategies available in narrative criticism,"[107] my book will take into account the historical context of the Second Temple Judaism. I will try to demonstrate this in chapter 2 of the present book. Secondly, unlike Byers's book which focuses on the inseparable relation between John's theology (and Christology) and its ecclesiology through the divine-human participation accommodated by the oneness of the *Shema*, my book attempts at constructing a framework (what I call the *Shema* framework) in order to help modern readers in reading the Gospel's oneness theology. I try to demonstrate this point using John 10 as a sample in chapter 4.

The *Shema* in John's Gospel Against its Backgrounds in Second Temple Judaism

This study is a dissertation submitted to Duke University by Lori Ann Robinson Baron in 2015. In this dissertation, Baron tries to "argue that the *Shema* is more central to the Christology and historical setting of John's Gospel than to any other New Testament writing, that John makes *more* of the *Shema* than do the Synoptic authors who cite it."[108] In doing so, Baron dedicated four chapters (chapters 2 to 5) exploring the influence of the *Shema* in the Old Testament, the Second Temple Literatures, and New Testament.[109] In chapter 6, Baron started her investigation of the influence of the *Shema* on the Gospel of John. Her investigation and arguments can be summarized as follows:

---

107. Byers, *Ecclesiology and Theosis*, 19
108. Baron, "The *Shema* in John's Gospel," 3
109. Baron, "The *Shema* in John's Gospel," 8–283

The Shema and John 10

Two-level Drama

Baron started her chapter 6 by surveying the works of scholars like C. K. Barrett, Birger Gerhardsson, C. T. R. Hayward, Johannes Beutler, Frédéric Manns, and Richard Bauckham on the topic. [110] After the survey, she concludes that those scholars neither paid much attention on the *Shema* in the Gospel (e.g., Gerhardsson) nor elaborated and explored its significance against its historical background (e.g., Barrett, Hayward, Manns). One important aspect was not addressed by them and given special attention in Baron's study is the historical context of the Gospel in relation with the *Shema*.[111] What Baron means by the historical context is to read the Gospel narrative as a two-level drama as proposed by Martyn.[112] According to her, "John's use of the *Shema* has a polemic and apologetic intent: the Fourth evangelist deploys the *Shema* in order to legitimate his community's confession of Christ, a confession which has gotten them expelled from the Jewish community."[113]

The Shema *and its theme in John 5, 8, and 10*

Baron starts her investigation of the *Shema* from John 5 which she identifies as "the first in a series of dramatic confrontations between Jesus and various groups of Jewish opponents."[114] Agreeing with Martyn, Baron reads this passage "as part of John's two-level drama" which explains the reason for the persecution experienced by Christian Jews—that is because they [the Christian Jews] worship Jesus as a second god!"[115] Baron believes it is very likely that the Christian Jews (the Johannine Community) were incorporating the *Shema* into the language of divine agency in reading

---

110. Baron, "The *Shema* in John's Gospel," 286–94.
111. Baron, "The *Shema* in John's Gospel," 287–8, 294.
112. Baron, "The *Shema* in John's Gospel," 284, 288.
113. In this case, Baron indebted to Martyn's two-level drama, see Baron, "The *Shema* in John's Gospel," 287, 294.
114. See Baron, "The *Shema* in John's Gospel," 296.
115. Baron, "The *Shema* in John's Gospel," 298.

The Shema and the Oneness Language in the Gospel of John

their expulsion experience back to Jesus' conflict with the (non-Christian) Jews.[116]

There are at least four connections between John 5 and the *Shema*. Firstly, John 5 presents Jesus to be equal with God. In this passage, Jesus is accused of making himself equal to God, not by means of calling God, His father (because the idea permeates Judaism through and through; e.g., Isa 63:16; Mal 2:10; Philo, *Decal.* 1:64; *Legat.* 1:115; *Mut.* 1:205; *Decal.* 1:8, 64; Tob 13:3–4), but by calling God as His *own* father and by doing what God does, especially on the Sabbath (cf. Aristob. 5:11–12; Philo, *Leg.* 1:5–7, 16–18; *Cher.* 86–90).[117] Jesus denied such an accusation by saying that he was not making himself equal to God, but he was bestowed such an equality by God himself.[118] In other words, Jesus is not claiming himself to be an independent deity or a rival to God, but a unique Son, who is *one* with God—probably alluding to the *Shema*.[119]

Secondly, the presence of and the emphasis on the word "hearing." Baron argues that "'hearing' in John recalls the Deuteronomic command to hear and obey YHWH (Deut 6:4), but rather than God, it is Jesus who must be heard."[120] And interestingly, Baron explains, "for John, those who hear and obey Jesus recognize him as the Prophet like Moses who is uniquely one with the Father, and therefore, they—believers in Jesus, not "the Jews"—are the ones who truly love God."[121] Thirdly, the importance of the word "love" in John 5. Although Baron is not completely certain that the word "love" in this passage is an echo of Deut. 6:5, she points out that there are at least three points suggesting the connection.[122] Those three points are: 1) The evidence from the Second Temple period shows that Deut 6:5 "was understood to be the statement

---

116. Baron, "The *Shema* in John's Gospel," 303
117. Baron, "The *Shema* in John's Gospel," 298–9
118. Baron, "The *Shema* in John's Gospel," 299, 304
119. Baron, "The *Shema* in John's Gospel," 304
120. Baron, "The *Shema* in John's Gospel," 307
121. Baron, "The *Shema* in John's Gospel," 310
122. Baron, "The *Shema* in John's Gospel," 311

The Shema and John 10

par excellence summarizing the command to love God"[123] 2) The presence of and emphases on the hearing motif and God's uniqueness as previously mentioned.[124] 3) The theme of life which will be discussed later.[125] Fourthly, the theme of life which reminds the readers of the Gospel of the result of obeying the commandments as summed up in the *Shema*.[126]

The second passage examined by Baron is John 8. According to Baron, just like John 5, this passage contains the themes of oneness, hearing, love, and life.[127] On the theme of oneness, Baron notes that the Gospel of John "uses the language of witness and testimony to describe Jesus' unity with the Father."[128] In this case, Jesus makes God His witness in order to fulfil the requirement of the Mosaic Law (e.g., Num 35:30; Deut 17:6; 19:15).[129] Another important point highlighting the theme of oneness is the use of the "I am" statement by Jesus referring to his unity with the Father.[130] The use of the "I am" statement here is very likely an echo of the monotheistic revelation of YHWH and the *Shema*.[131] In addition, the depiction of Jesus being objected and almost stoned is an indication that his claim has anything to do with the Jewish notion of divine unity.[132]

On the hearing motif, Baron shows there is an interesting observation need to be noted here. On the one hand, John 8 presents Jesus as the one embodies the *Shema* by hearing and obeying the commands of the Father. On the other hand, the Jews are portrayed as the ones cannot hear the voice of Jesus indicating their

---

123. Baron, "The *Shema* in John's Gospel," 311
124. Baron, "The *Shema* in John's Gospel," 311
125. Baron, "The *Shema* in John's Gospel," 311
126. Baron, "The *Shema* in John's Gospel," 311–4
127. Baron, "The *Shema* in John's Gospel," 316
128. Baron, "The *Shema* in John's Gospel," 316
129. Baron, "The *Shema* in John's Gospel," 317
130. Baron, "The *Shema* in John's Gospel," 319–20
131. Baron, "The *Shema* in John's Gospel," 321–5
132. Baron, "The *Shema* in John's Gospel," 325

The Shema *and the Oneness Language in the Gospel of John*

origin which is not from the Father.[133] The same can be seen in the loving motif of this passage in which the Jews reject to love Jesus because they are not from the Father (8:42).[134] The last theme, that is the life, is also connected to the *Shema* as those two are explicitly linked in Deuteronomy.[135] In John 8:51–53, Jesus, not Moses, is presented as the source of life just like God described in the *Shema* of the Deuteronomic tradition.[136]

The third important passage, John 10, is also related to the *Shema* in the same way where the theme of oneness, hearing, loving, and life occur throughout the passage. The theme of hearing can be seen in the acts of hearing performed by the sheep. The sheep will hear the voice of the true Shepherd and not the thieves and bandits.[137] The theme of oneness, John 10—both the Shepherd discourse (10:1–22) and its second part (10:22–42), is articulated through the unity of Jesus and the Father.[138] Echoing Ezek 34 (and other second temple texts; e.g., Jer 23:3; Ps 23:1; 80:2; Sir 18:13; Zech 10:3; Isa 40:11; Mic 7:14; Philo, *Agr.* 50–53; *Post.* 67–68) the Shepherd discourse presents Jesus, just like YHWH in Judaism, as the good Shepherd of Israel.[139] In the second part of John 10, the most striking oneness language is found in verse 30 where Jesus claims that "I and the Father are one." Baron agrees with Bauckham that the use of neuter ἕν instead of masculine εἷς is a necessary grammatical adaptation without compromising the oneness of the *Shema*.[140]

The love theme is presented in the reciprocal relationship between Jesus and the Father; that is, as noted by Baron, "the Father's love for Jesus and Jesus' obedience to the Father's command

---

133. Baron, "The *Shema* in John's Gospel," 326–7
134. Baron, "The *Shema* in John's Gospel," 327–8
135. Baron, "The *Shema* in John's Gospel," 328
136. Baron, "The *Shema* in John's Gospel," 329–30
137. Baron, "The *Shema* in John's Gospel," 334–5
138. Baron, "The *Shema* in John's Gospel," 335
139. Baron, "The *Shema* in John's Gospel," 335–48
140. Baron, "The *Shema* in John's Gospel," 349–50

The Shema and John 10

reflect a similar relationship."[141] In addition, the love theme is also stressed by the fourth evangelist in Jesus' act of laying down his life.[142] The theme of life echoes the gift of life and protection promised by YHWH to those (Israel) who hear his voice and obey his commandments as stated in the *Shema*. Here in John 10 the life is specified as the eternal life given to those who hear the voice of Jesus.[143]

The Shema *and its themes in the Farewell Discourse*

In the beginning of chapter 7 of her work, Baron states that "the Johannine references to the *Shema* and its themes of hearing, oneness, love, and life, are concentrated in the Farewell Discourse (John 13:31–17:26), where the focus becomes Jesus' interactions with his disciples"[144] The *Shema* in John 14–15 can be identified by the activities YHWH and Jesus perform together as one such as choosing a people, loving a people, commanding love, issuing commandments, and giving life.[145]

In John 17 the word ἕν from 10:30 reappears five times (17:11, 21, 22 [2x], 23) describing both Jesus' unity with the Father and Jesus' unity with his people.[146] Some important observations on the unity of Jesus and the Father in John 17 are: 1) Jesus, as the one sent by the only true God, is entrusted by the Father to impart eternal life (17:2); 2) The expression "to know" God instead of to love indicating the possible allusion to Deuteronomy (e.g., Deut 4:39; cf. 7:9; 9:3, 6; 29:6); 3) The affirmation of Jesus' unity with the Father even before the existence of the world (17:5; cf. 17:24).[147] On the unity of Jesus and His disciples, Baron argues that the fourth evangelist uses Ezekiel's terms which echo the oneness of the *Sh-*

141. Baron, "The *Shema* in John's Gospel," 355
142. Baron, "The *Shema* in John's Gospel," 357
143. Baron, "The *Shema* in John's Gospel," 357–9
144. Baron, "The *Shema* in John's Gospel," 362
145. Baron, "The *Shema* in John's Gospel," 365–72
146. Baron, "The *Shema* in John's Gospel," 374
147. Baron, "The *Shema* in John's Gospel," 376–7

ema to communicate the unity of the people and the witnessing responsibility of the unified people.[148] Applying Martyn approach, Baron believes that the passage has anything to do with "those who are alive at the time of the writing and experiencing persecution."[149]

The last passage of the farewell discourse examined by Baron is John 13. Baron carefully points out the importance of the love command showing the fourth evangelist's awareness of the singular commandment of the Mosaic Law in Deuteronomy.[150] The love commandment given by Jesus functions not only as an allusion to the love commandment in the *Shema*, but it also marks the beginning of a new era in which the *Shema* has been transformed around the relationship between Jesus and the Father.[151]

The Shema *in the Johannine crucifixion, Anti-Judaism, and the Prologue.*

In chapter 8 of her work, Baron suggest that the *Shema* has something to do with Jesus, crucifixion, the anti-Judaism narrative, and the Prologue. Regarding Jesus' crucifixion, Baron argues that it is driven by the Jews' accusation that Jesus making himself king, which relates to the idea of Jesus' unity with God, the Father.[152] And on the anti-Judaism narrative, Baron suggests that "John deploys the *Shema* in a rhetorical move that reverses the historical situation, creating insiders of the Johannine community, who have been forced outside of Jewish life."[153] The suggestion simply means that the anti-Judaism narrative has to be read not in terms of anti-Semitism, but in the context of the Jews' rejection of Jesus' unity with the Father (the Johannine reading of the *Shema*) which is

---

148. Baron, "The *Shema* in John's Gospel," 378–80
149. Baron, "The *Shema* in John's Gospel," 377
150. Baron, "The *Shema* in John's Gospel," 389
151. Baron, "The *Shema* in John's Gospel," 405
152. Baron, The *Shema* in John's Gospel, 408
153. Baron, The *Shema* in John's Gospel, 409

The Shema and John 10

also experienced by the Johannine community.[154] In the end of her work, Baron states the importance of the *Shema* for the Prologue. According to her, the Prologue gains "force and clarity in the light of John's Christological reworking of the *Shema* in the rest of the Gospel."[155] The unity of Jesus with the Father and the demand for loving Him in the Prologue fulfills what is stated in the *Shema*.[156]

Comments on Baron's Approach

Like Byers, Baron must be commended for her careful treatment of the relation between the oneness language of the Gospel with the *Shema*. Simply put, what these two works have done is an advancement in the study of the oneness language of the Gospel of John. I must say (again) that I totally agree with their premise that the *Shema* is an interpretive key for the oneness language of the Gospel. However, these two works are methodologically different. Unlike Byers, Baron has been considering and incorporating the historical context (she clearly has benefited much from Martyn's study) into her analysis of the *Shema* in the Gospel.

Frankly, my book will benefit much from Baron's findings in her works. However, our studies will differ in these two particular ways: 1) As previously stated, my work concerns not only with the oneness language against the background of the Gospel, but primarily with providing a framework for understanding the oneness language of the Gospel; 2) I really appreciate Baron's efforts in examining the historical context of the oneness language of the Gospel. Just like Baron, I will also take into considerations the importance of the historical context. But, different from her, I am not convinced by Martyn's two-level drama proposal. I am more convinced that the Jamnian Judaism[157] and the destruction of the Temple are the historical context for understanding the oneness

---

154. Baron, The *Shema* in John's Gospel, 410–21

155. Baron, The *Shema* in John's Gospel, 421

156. Baron, The *Shema* in John's Gospel, 421

157. I am more convinced that both the Gospel of John and the Jamnian Judaism are addressing the same problem, rather than engaging each other.

The Shema and the Oneness Language in the Gospel of John

language of the Gospel. I will try to explain this point in chapter 2 of the present book.

Conclusion

The four studies surveyed are indeed impressive and insightful for Johannine scholarship, particularly on the oneness language of the Gospel. However, as previously mentioned, I have some reservations for those studies. As for the works of Appold and Tong, I believe, the background and foreground aspects (these two terms will be explained later in chapter 2) of the oneness motif of the Gospel of John have to be taken into account.[158] Some scholars have rightly surmised that the oneness motif for the New Testament writings, including the Fourth Gospel, are closely connected with the Jewish notion of the oneness of God or monotheism in the Second Temple period. According to Larry Hurtado, Jewish monotheism in the Second Temple period is unique in the way the Jews understand their God as "sovereign God and the only one compared to other entities."[159] Similarly, N.T. Wright understands Jewish monotheism according to two basic criteria; that of creation and election.[160] Monotheism, under the creation criterion, means that God is known as the sole creator of the universe (Gen 1). In this case, Jewish monotheism is seen as deriving principally from God's revelation. The core of election and monotheism produces a concept called covenantal monotheism. It simply means that the God of the universe has chosen Israel to be his people (Gen 12).

Bauckham, who holds the same view as Hurtado and Wright, argues that Jewish monotheism is inevitably strict.[161] This strictness can be seen through the exclusive worship dedicated to God

---

158. Davies, "Reflections on Aspects," 43–59; cf. Dunn, *Jesus Remembered*, 255–92.

159. Hurtado, "First Century," 12–3; Hurtado, *One God*, 17–92; Hurtado, *Lord Jesus*, 29–47.

160. Wright, *The New Testament*, 248–52.

161. Bauckham, *Jesus and the God*, 3.

The Shema and John 10

as the sole creator and the ruler over all.[162] There are no other figures, including angels and patriarchs, who are worthy of being worshipped besides God.[163] That is why first century Jews had difficulty agreeing with Jewish Christians who believed in Jesus' deity. However, the Jewish Christians never thought of abandoning their monotheistic belief when they believed in Jesus' deity. They, as Christians, rather believed that God has revealed himself to his people through the figure of Jesus. In this case, Jesus is recognized as God because he "shares" God's unique identity, such as his sovereignty over all things, participation in creation, etc.[164] In short, for them, God's identity as sole creator and ruler is revealed in Jesus.[165]

At a closer look, it can be said that both the Jews and Christians share the same concept of oneness—that is relational and revelational oneness. And more importantly, all of these points are summed up in the Jewish creed called the *Shema* (Deut 6.4–9). The *Shema* is not only Jewish most important prayer and creed but it also acts as the identity marker for the Jews in the Second Temple period, as will be demonstrated in chapter 2. This book chooses John 10 in order to demonstrate how the *Shema* influences the Gospel's understanding of the oneness motif. John 10 has been chosen due to its unique features: 1) It explicitly presents an apparently unique relationship between Jesus and the Father in referring to its oneness motif which is scattered all over the Gospel; 2) It has all elements of the *Shema* (monotheism, election-covenant, and eschatology) in its oneness language usages; 3) It is a very rich, imaginative, and interesting passage. John 10 has also been chosen due to its—full of imageries and allusions to the Old Testament and Hellenistic culture—which no one has (yet) ever made serious or thorough studies on the connection between its oneness motif and the *Shema*.

---

162. Bauckham, *Jesus and the God*, 11–13, 18.
163. Bauckham, *Jesus and the God*, 14–17.
164. Bauckham, *Jesus and the God*, 20–31.
165. Bauckham, *Jesus and the God*, 31–57.

The Shema *and the Oneness Language in the Gospel of John*

As for the work of Byers, I think it is important to consider the importance of the historical context of the oneness language of the Gospel. Although the work of Baron has demonstrated the importance of the historical context, this book will differ from hers in identifying the context. Rather than following Martyn's two-level drama proposal, I am more convinced that the Jamnian Judaism and the destruction of the Temple are the context in question. Moreover, different from those two works, this book will concern primarily with constructing a framework in reading the oneness language in the Gospel.

2

The *Shema* as the Framework

THE AWARENESS THAT THE Gospel of John was closely related to Judaism was already demonstrated by some scholars in the beginning of the last century.[1] However, it had not been widely accepted until C. H. Dodd. Through his publications—*The Historical Tradition in the Fourth Gospel* and *The Interpretation of the Fourth Gospel*—he challenged the Johannine scholars to (re)consider the importance of Judaism, besides the *Hermetica*, in the study of the Gospel of John.[2] Since then, the idea that Judaism, the Old Testament[3] and other Jewish writings (Qumran,[4] Philo,[5] Jewish Wisdom,[6] etc.), played an important role for understanding the theology of John's Gospel—including its oneness motif—was

1. Smith, "John," 99.

2. See Davies, "In Memoriam," Charles Harold Dodd, 1884–1973," in *New Testament Studies* 20 (1973–74).

3. E.g., Schuchard, *Scripture within Scripture*; Hanson, *The Prophetic Gospel*; Menken, *Old Testament Quotations*.

4. E.g., Charlesworth (Ed.), *John and the Dead Sea Scrolls*; Coloe and Thatcher (Eds.), *John, Qumran, and the Dead Sea Scrolls*; Tukasi, *Determinism and Petitionary Prayer*.

5. E.g., Carmichael, *The Story of Creation*; Borgen, *The Gospel*; Bennema, *The Power of Saving Wisdom*.

6. E.g., Smith, *Jewish Wisdom*; Bennema, *The Power of Saving Wisdom*.

The Shema as the Framework

gradually acknowledged.⁷ Perhaps, it is still expedient to attempt to construct a framework from within Judaism for understanding the oneness motif of the Gospel of John.

W. D. Davies has convincingly demonstrated that the Jewish background of the Gospel of John is Second Temple Judaism and the destruction of the Temple.⁸ The former refers to the theology and tradition the Gospel inherited from,⁹ while the latter to its historical setting. Before proceeding, some clarifications need to be made in advance. First, Second Temple Judaism will be understood in terms of the common belief of the Jews of the period, the common Judaism, as suggested by E. P. Sanders in his *Judaism: Practice and Belief*.¹⁰

This section will focus only on the relevant issue: the *Shema* as the common belief in Second Temple Judaism. Secondly, about the destruction of the Temple, the response of Jamnian Judaism to the destruction will be taken into account in order to evaluate how the event influences the oneness theme in John's Gospel.

---

7. See Smith, *John*; Keener, *The Gospel*, 171.

8. Davies, "Reflections," 43–59; Köstenberger, "Destruction," 88, 94.

9. Others, like Jack P. Lewis, S. Brown, M. Black, E. C. Colwell, etc., include the language used by the Fourth Evangelist into this category (they call it the Semitic Background). e.g., Lewis, "The Semitic Background," 97–110; Brown, "From Burney to Black," 323–39; Colwell, *The Greek*.

10. It is evident that there was no single form of Judaism in the Second Temple period. It is rather appropriate to speak of Judaisms, in plural, than Judaism, in singular (Wright, *The New Testament*, 244; Keener, *John*, 181). The most often cited source for this is Josephus, of which reveals the existence of at least four different Jewish groups or sects during this era—there were Pharisees, Sadducees, Essenes and Zealots (*Ant.* 1 3 .1 7 1; *War* 2.1 1 8). This fact is well identified and discussed by some scholars, like Jacob Neusner (Neusner, *Judaism: the Evidence of the Misnah*; *Messiah in Context*; *Judaism in the Beginning*; *Judaism When Christianity Began*; *Judaisms and their Messiahs*), R. T. Herford (Herford, *Judaism in the New Testament*), and Alan Segal (Segal, *Brown Judaic Studies*), but to mention some. Regardless that fact, Sanders argues that it is still possible to speak of the common practices and beliefs, e.g., belief in one God, the covenant, the sacrificial system, etc., among the varieties (Sanders, *Judaism: Practice and Belief*).

31

The Gospel of John and Common Judaism

As mentioned earlier, common Judaism of the Second Temple period is the Jewish background of the Gospel of John. Therefore, it is important to understand how the Gospel's oneness language and motif are shaped and influenced by it. To begin with, Ephraim E. Urbach's comment is worth noting here. He states that monotheism was "the belief common to all Jews at the beginning of the first century" which means the Jews believed that "their God was the only God and their religion was the only true religion" (see *Ant.* 5. 1, 27, 112; *Sib. Or.* 3.629).[11] Sanders has rightly insisted that monotheism was not only a common belief, it was also the most important belief of the Jews in this period (see Philo, *Decal.* 65).[12] Wright goes as far as to claim that "all accounts of Jewish theology rightly focus on monotheism."[13] He also argues that for the Jews of this period, monotheism was not a philosophical speculation, but a practical matter.[14] This belief was seen as the embodiment of the first commandment given by God himself (Exod 20:3).[15] It was also treated as the application of the *Shema* recited [twice] daily (*m. Berakhot* 1:1–4)[16] by the Jews of this period (*m. Tamid* 5:1).[17] In this context, there are two things to be noted. First, in the context of the *Shema* and the first commandment, the God of Israel is known as the only true God—the creator of and the ruler over the universe[18]—who is superior to any other beings (3 Macc

---

11. Urbach, "Self-Isolation or Self-Affirmation," 233.
12. Sanders, *Judaism*, 242; Moore, *Judaism*, 360–1.
13. Wright, *The New Testament*, 248.
14. Wright, *Paul and the Faithfulness*, 619–23.
15. Sanders, *Judaism*, 242.
16. Tan, "Jesus and the *Shema*," 2680; "The *Shema* and the Early Christianity," 181–2; Gerhardsson, *The Shema*, 10.
17. Wright, *Paul and the Faithfulness*, 624; *The New Testament*, 248; Sanders, *Judaism*, 242, 247–9; Dunn, *The Partings*, 26–7.
18. Cf. Moore, "The Search," 137–8; Hurtado, *How on Earth*, 120–2. Marianne M. Thompson finds that both in Josephus and Philo the idea that God is the creator is linked with the notion that He is the Father of Israel (see Thompson, *The Promise*, 48–53. This is interesting since the Gospel of John

The Shema as the Framework

7:9; 1QS 10:12; 11QBer 3; 1QM 18:7; *Spec.* 1:30; *Decal.* 61; *Mut.* 29).[19] It means that monotheism in this period is understood and characterized through what God does—creating and ruling the world. This is the reason why the God of Israel is the only one to be exclusively worshipped.[20] This fact is supported by Bauckham[21] and Hurtado, who have decisively shown that although there were many intermediary figures acknowledged and respected in Judaism of this period, they all were never worshipped by the people. Thus, secondly, monotheism in this period is unique in its nature. It should not be understood numerically, but uniquely.[22] By "unique," I mean monotheism in this period is to be understood as the oneness in the identity of God—revealing the Identity of God as the creator and ruler—and its relation to his people.[23]

According to Thompson and Bauckham, this monotheism is the background for understanding the concept of God in John's Gospel. [24] It also certainly influences the oneness language in the Gospel.[25] To the Gospel, the authority to create, rule, judge, and redeem the world belongs to God alone. That is why the Jews accuse Jesus as a blasphemer for what he has done, including "claiming" himself to be "equal with God" (John 5:18; 8:59; 10:31–33; cf. 11:8).[26] Interestingly, although Jesus is depicted as being accused

---

employs the same ideas too; that the Father is also the creator.

19. Moore, *Judaism*, 361; Wright, *The New Testament*, 248–9.

20. Thompson, *The God of the Gospel*, 54; Andreas J. Köstenberger, *A Theology of John's Gospel*, 356–7; Dunn, *Did the First Christians*, 62; *The Partings*, 27–8; Sanders, *Judaism*, 247.

21. Bauckham, *The Climax*, 118–49; "the 'Most High' God," 39–53.

22. Hurtado, *Lord Jesus Christ*, 42–4.

23. Bauckham, "Monotheism and Christology," 164; *God Crucified*, 7; Hurtado, "First-Century Jewish Monotheism,", 3–26.

24. Thompson, *The God*, 17–55; Bauckham, "Monotheism and Christology", 148; cf. Thompson, *The Promise*, 53.

25. Byers, "Johannine Theosis," 108–10

26. Köstenberger, *A Theology*, 357; Bauckham, "Monotheism and Christology", 149; McGrath, *John's Apologetic*, 78, 80–102. Here, McGrath's remark is worth noting. He argues that, "God could appoint agents, who would represent Him and bears His full authority. It was someone who had not appointed by

The Shema and John 10

as such by the Jews on several occasions and for several reasons, the Gospel never addresses or presents Jesus as a competing god of the God of Israel.[27] This is because the evangelist of the Fourth Gospel incorporates his oneness language with the unique features of the *Shema*—relational and revelational oneness. The Relational oneness is applied to the relationship between Jesus and the Father. That is why the Gospel describes that Jesus' authority comes from God, the Father (John 5:17, 19; 8:26, 38). Jesus comes to the world because he is sent by the Father (John 5:36; 7:29; 17:4).[28] The Revelational oneness is applied to Jesus' works in revealing the identity of God, the Father (John 7:28; 8:26).[29] Some scholars have used the term christological monotheism to describe the application of this (Jewish) monotheism to the Gospel.[30]

The other aspects of Jewish monotheism (the *Shema*) of this period are the concept of election and covenant. The Jews believe that the only true God confessed in the *Shema* is not only the creator of and the ruler over the universe, but also the God who elects Israel among other nations to be His own people (Gen 12, 15, 17, etc.).[31] Through His covenant with Abraham, God binds himself with Israel in an everlasting relationship (see Gen 12; Deut 27–30; Jub 12.19–20).[32] Dunn states that this makes Israel "to be a people

---

God that equality with God became problematic and even blasphemous; and it was into this latter category that 'the Jews' placed Jesus" (78); cf. Baron, "The *Shema* in John's Gospel," 284–94

27. Davies, *Rhetoric and Reference*, 129–32; cf. Bauckham, *Jesus and the God*, 147; J. Michaels, *The Gospel of John*, 601; Byers, *Ecclesiology and Theosis*, 36; Baron, "The *Shema* in John's Gospel," 298

28. Appold, *The Oneness Motif*, 19; Davies, *Rhetoric*, 163–7; cf. McGrath, *John's Apologetic*, 103–16.

29. Bauckham, "Monotheism and Christology",152–3; Appold, *The Oneness Motif*, 20–34; cf. McGrath, *John's Apologetic*, 71–9; Cowan, "The Father and Son," 115–35.

30. This point will be fully discussed in chapter 3 and 4.

31. Flusser, *Judaism (Vol. 2)*, 8; Wright, *The New Testament*, 259; Dunn, *The Partings*, 29–32; Moore, "The Search," 138–9.

32. Neusner, *Judaism when Christianity*, 91–3; Wright, *The New Testament*, 26–1; Dunn, *The Partings*, 29.

The Shema as the Framework

separated to and for the Lord."[33] To be God's people means both having a privilege of inheriting his promises and living his legacy. As repeatedly emphasized in the Jewish writings,[34] especially the book of Deuteronomy, the God of Israel will fulfil His promises to the children of Abraham, Isaac and Jacob—the promise of blessings, land, and honor among the nations (e.g., Deut 1:8, 11; 6:10–12; 29:12–13).[35] This privilege is followed by the assurance that their God will always be faithful and will intervene in history for the sake of His people.[36] But, on the other hand, their God demands them to follow His legacy—based on Torah (e.g., Jub 22:16; Bar 3:36–4:4).[37] They must maintain their holiness among the Gentiles in order to restore the fallen world.[38] This explains many groups in this period, e.g., Qumran, Essenes, and Zealots, separate themselves in order to maintain such holiness before their God.[39] And for the same reason some groups became involved in the revolts of this period, e.g. Hasmonean revolt (BC 167 to BC 160), and the 66 to 70 Revolt.[40] In connection with the *Shema*, the election of and covenant made with Israel signify the importance of the oneness of God, which is seen in the oneness of His people.[41]

The concept of election and covenant is a central theme of John's Gospel.[42] In addition to that, it also obviously effects the use of the oneness language of the Gospel. The election of the disciples in John 1:35–51 is a starting point for the theology of election in the Gospel of John. As Israel is elected by the one God to restore the world, the disciples are also elected to do the same (John

33. Dunn, *The Partings*, 29.
34. Wright, *The New Testament*, 262–72.
35. Wright, *The New Testament*, 261.
36. Wright, *The New Testament*, 250–1.
37. Dunn, *The Partings*, 32–42.
38. Sanders, *Judaism*, 286; Flusser, *Judaism*, 8–10; Wright, *The New Testament*, 260.
39. Wright, *The New Testament*, 261–2.
40. Sanders, *Judaism*, 280–9; Wright, *The New Testament*, 261–2.
41. Bauckham, "Monotheism and Christology," 164.
42. Ferreira, *Johannine Ecclesiology*, 112.

1:40–1, 49–51; 13:31–35; 15). Chennattu explains that the election of the disciples to be the one people of God in John's Gospel represents the covenant between God and his people—as presented in the Old Testament and Second Temple Judaism.[43] He asserts that discipleship is a means to reveal God's identity to the disciples in order to incorporate them into one new covenant community.[44] Another expression of the concept of election and covenant in the Gospel of John is the image of the bridegroom (John 3:29). McWhirter argues that the image is an allusion to a theme found in the Jewish writings, both the Old Testament and the writings of the Second Temple Period.[45] She proceeds to explicate the imagery as signifying the relationship between the one Messiah and His people—or the covenant between them.[46] An important concept of the covenant can also be seen in the imagery of the vine and its branch (John 15). The imagery underlines the importance of the relationship between the true vine [God] and its true branch [the true Israel]—who are one in covenantal relationship.[47] Whoever lives in the covenant with God, he/she will live (John 15:7–17).[48] Interestingly, there is a transposition from "God-his people relationship" to "Jesus-his people relationship" in this imagery. Then, it may be true that this imagery is used to not only reveal the identity of the true branch (God's people), but also the (one) God himself in Jesus. In addition, the concepts of election and covenant are more extensively described in chapters 10 and 17. In John 10, which is an allusion of Ezek. 32 (and Psalms 23), the election and covenant are made to gather the people/sheep of God into one under one shepherd (John 10:16; 11:52). It might be true that the phrase "one flock, one shepherd" emphasizes the importance of monotheism

43. Chennattu, *Johannine Discipleship*, 59–61, 68–80, 180–93.
44. Chennattu, *Johannine Discipleship*, 139.
45. McWhirter, *The Bridegroom*, 46–78.
46. McWhirter, *The Bridegroom*, Ch. 3–5; cf. Sohn, *The Divine Election*, 241–2.
47. Stevick, *Jesus and His Own*, 184–200.
48. Stevick, *Jesus and His Own*, 200–16; Baron gives interesting notes on the life theme in the Gospel is closely related to the *Shema*, see Baron, "The *Shema* in John's Gospel," 311–4, 316, 334–5

in the theology of election and covenant in the Gospel of John. Jan G. van der Watt in his extensive study on the theme of family in the Gospel of John considers John 10 as alluding to the relationship between the King and His family.[49] This familial relationship suggests the intimacy of the covenantal relationship between the one God and his people.[50] Furthermore, Bauckham argues that John 17 is, theologically and literary, the embodiment of John 10. According to him, the basis for the unity of the disciples in John 17 is John 10.30—the unity of Jesus and God (the Father).[51] It also means that the disciples are to be separated/consecrated from the world for God.[52] In addition, Jesus in John 17 can also be perceived as performing his priestly office.[53] On the one hand, he represents the only true God before the only people of God. And on the other, he prays on behalf of the only people of God to their only God.

Monotheism is also the mother of Jewish eschatology in this period.[54] The people of God were oppressed, the Temple was defiled, and the promise land was occupied by pagans.[55] This situation raised many questions regarding the sovereignty of their God and their status as His people. The initial answer to the question was that the situation was seen as a punishment from God because

---

49. van der Watt, *Family of the King*, 54–92, 158–60; In her work (especially chapter 2), Baron argues that the language of the *Shema* is primarily based on the language of ancient political treaties between a king and his vassals. She further shows that such a language is also found in the Gospel of John with a special reference to Jesus, see Baron, "The *Shema* in John's Gospel," 338, 364–409

50. van der Watt, *Family of the King*, 159–60; cf. Byers, *Ecclesiology and Theosis*, 106, 179

51. Bauckham, *The Testimony*, 265–6; cf. Dodd, *The Interpretation*, 418–9.

52. Bauckham, *The Testimony*, 268. In addition, Keener notes that the "knowing motif" in 17.3 fits biblical tradition of the covenantal relationship. See Keener, *The Gospel of John (vol. 2)*, 1054.

53. Attridge, "How Priestly," 1–14; cf. Keener, *The Gospel of John (vol. 2)*, 1051; Brown, *The Gospel (vol. 2)* (Garden City: Doubleday, 1970), 747.

54. Wright, *The New Testament*, 272, 299–301; *Paul and the Faithfulness*, 1045–6.

55. Flusser, *Judaism*, 29.

The Shema and John 10

they had sinned against their God.⁵⁶ In this case, sins against God could be regarded as a violation of the *Shema*⁵⁷. They needed to repent in order to gain deliverance from God as promised in the Old Testament (e.g., Isa 40:1-2; Jer 31:31, 34, 38, 40). Some sects, like the Zealots, believed that the problem came from the pagans. Thus, they must get rid of the pagans through whatever means necessary.⁵⁸ Other sects, like the Pharisees, believed that the oppression was the punishment for their failure to observe the Torah, tradition and purity (cf. *Ant.* 18:12). Hence, they must obey the Torah and observe the tradition and purity in order to be redeemed by God.⁵⁹ The answers were many and varied depending on the sects.⁶⁰ However, their hope was the same that their God will one day deliver them from this oppression and bring them back to Zion (e.g., Isa 32:22, 52:7-8).⁶¹ This hope is strengthened through the reading of the Exodus event (cf. Isa 45:1) in this period.⁶² It articulated the importance of the eschatological messiah (royal messiah), prophet, and high priest figure (cf. 1QSa 2:11-12, 14; 1QS 9:11; CD. 12:23-13:1; Bar. 39:7) as "savior figures who would deliver Israel from her pagan oppressors."⁶³

Jewish eschatology also influences the Gospel's eschatology and its oneness language. The eschatology of the Gospel focuses on the oneness of Jesus and the Father and the redemption of the one people of God. In John 1:19-21 John the Baptist is asked about his identity, whether he is the messiah or not. He rejects not only the eschatological messiah title, but also the title of the eschatological

56. Wright, *The New Testament*, 272-3; cf. Thettayil, *In Spirit and Truth*, 243.

57. Moore, *Judaism*, 465.

58. Wright, *The New Testament*, 302.

59. Wright, *The New Testament*, 194-5.

60. Neusner, "The Pharisaic Agenda," 315-8; Wright, *The New Testament*, 262.

61. Horbury, *Jewish Messianism*, 40, 64-8; Wright, *The New Testament*, 269, 278, 300-1; cf. Talmon, "The Concept of Māšîaḥ" 107-8.

62. Cf. Bauckham, "Messianism," 44, 46.

63. Bauckham, "Messianism", 39; Sanders, *Judaism*, 295-7; Flusser, *Judaism*, 29-35; Wright, *The New Testament*, 299-301, 307-20.

The Shema as the Framework

prophet.[64] Through what Jesus has done in his ministry,[65] the evangelist identifies Him with the figures of the eschatological prophet and messiah sent by the one God.[66] As the eschatological prophet, Jesus is expected to deliver and restore God's people from oppression and bring about the new exodus (see John 6–7).[67] As the eschatological messiah,[68] Jesus will rule and reign over God's people on behalf of God as promised in the Old Testament—that God will enact the kingdom of David forever (John 1:43–51; 12:34; 4 Ezra 7:2; 2 Bar 30:1).[69] It corresponds with the Christological titles in the Gospel of John—the Son of God, the King of Israel, and the Son of Man. The Son of God refers to Israel in the Old Testament, which means that Jesus represents, on the one hand, Israel as the chosen one (cf. Gen 12; 15; 17) and God who will

---

64. After examining some Jewish sources, both from the Second Temple period and rabbinic writings, Bauckham even suggests that John 1:19–21 might be related to three eschatological figures: the Davidic royal Messiah, the eschatological Prophet, and the eschatological High Priest. See Bauckham, "Messianism," 36–39.

65. Peter W. Ensor argues that the works Jesus done are revelation of the identity of God. He also argues that the Gospel of John presents Jesus only does what God asks Him to do. See Ensor, *Jesus and His Works*, chapters. 4 to 9

66. Bauckham, "Messianism," 63.

67. Brunson, *Psalm 118*, 153–6; Bauckham, "Messianism", 53. Here, Appold (and probably Byers too, see Byers, *Ecclesiology and Theosis*, 32) misunderstands the eschatological prophet title given to Jesus by saying "those presuppositions do not derive from a prophetic Christology but rather from a Christology of oneness which identifies Jesus as the heavenly person who is one with God." There is nowhere in the Gospel of John Jesus is clearly presented protologically as understood by Appold. The evangelist always present Jesus eschatologically, including John 1 (the eschatological revelation of God in Jesus), of which the prophet title should be understood as God's act/ revelation to his people through Jesus.

68. I agree with John Ashton that "there is nothing inherently blasphemous in a claim to be the Messiah". Richard A. Horsley has provided data that there were many, like Judas son of Ezekias (4 BC) and Manahem (AD 66), regarded as messiahs without being accused as blasphemers. See Ashton, *Understanding*, 241; cf. Horsley, "'Messianic," 276–95; Beasley-Murray, *John*, 75.

69. Bauckham, "Messianism," 64–7; Ashton, *Understanding*, 255; cf. Pomykala, *The Davidic Dynasty*, Ch. 4–5; Baron, "The *Shema* in John's Gospel," 335–9,

The Shema and John 10

save His people on the other (cf. Pss 2; 4 Ezra 13; 1QSa 2:11–12).[70] The King of Israel, according to Bauckham, should not be distinguished from the King of the Jews which is the Davidic Messiah in Ps Sol 17:24—who will come and reign over God's people.[71] The same can be said about the title of the Son of Man which draws upon Dan 7:13–14—who is, in the Second Temple Judaism, also the Davidic Messiah.[72] Appold is right when he says that all those titles show the relationship of God [the Father] with Jesus. However, he is not convincing because he understands it protologically, rather than eschatologically.[73] All this shows that the eschatology of the Fourth Gospel is strongly influenced by the relational and revelational oneness of the *Shema*.

By way of summary, it is evident that the Gospel of John was greatly influenced by Judaism of the Second Temple period. The most influential element is the concept of monotheism—the embodiment of the first commandment and the *Shema*—which is common to all Jews of the time. Jewish monotheism of this period has predominantly shaped John's theology of God, of the people of God and of its eschatology as seen in the use of the latter's oneness language. This finding suggests that the *Shema* can be used as the framework for understanding John's theology in general and John 10 in particular.

---

70. Ashton, *Understanding*, 260-2; Hurtado, *Lord Jesus Christ*, 360-1; Bauckham, "Messianism," 58.

71. Bauckham, "Messianism," 59-60; cf. Ashton, *Understanding*, 262.

72. Burkett has provided a very useful survey on the history of the interpretation of the Son of [the] Man in the Gospel of John. Some scholars cited think that the Son of Man in John is an allusion to Daniel, but some other doubt that. For both supporting and dissenting views, see Burkett, *The Son of the Man*, 16-37. For some references regarding the connection of the Son of Man with the Apocalyptic Messiah of the Second Temple period, see Bauckham, "Messianism", 67; cf. Vanderkam, "Righteous One," 187.

73. Appold, *The Oneness Motif*, 55, 58, 78. To understand Jesus' oneness with the Father eschatologically means to see Jesus as the One who comes on behalf of God to save God's people.

The Gospel of John and the Destruction of the Temple

Lindars, in his commentary on the Gospel of John, asserts that "John is far too important to be merely derived from the continuation of Jewish ideas in the Church, and [it] demands actual contact with (contemporary) Judaism."[74] Louis Martyn in his *History and Theology in the Fourth Gospel* suggests that the Gospel of John was written as a response to Jamnian Judaism.[75] He conjectures that the Gospel of John (and all New Testament books) consists of both traditions and their interpretations.[76] The traditions refer to the materials common to both the Synoptic Gospels and John (and Paul). And the interpretations of the traditions are the unique elements of the overlapped-materials which are found only in the Gospel of John.[77] In other words, the fourth evangelist presents not only the historical events of Jesus' ministry, but also his own situation in his Gospel. Martyn calls it a two-level drama.[78] An example of this is found in John 9, where he argues that the story of the expulsion of the blind beggar recalls not only the historical event of Jesus' ministry,[79] but also the expulsion of the Jewish Christian in the evangelist's time (post-Jamnian).[80]

There are two things that can be said about Martyn's approach to the relation of the Gospel of John and Jamnian Judaism. The first is his remarkable contribution of spotting the importance of Jamnian Judaism to the Gospel of John. As said by Moody Smith

---

74. Lindars, *The Gospel*, 38. It is now widely accepted that the Gospel of John was written in during the time of Jamnian Judaism.

75. As previously mentioned, Baron incorporates Martyn's approach into her investigation see Baron, "The *Shema* in John's Gospel," 9, 287–8, 298, 315.

76. Martyn, *History and Theology*, 30.

77. Martyn, *History and Theology*, 30–1.

78. Martyn, *History and Theology*, 32.

79. Martyn, *History and Theology*, 35–45.

80. Martyn, *History and Theology*, 46–66; cf. Klink, *The Sheep of the Fold*, 116. Klink, following Smith's *Theology of the Gospel of John*, identifies the history part of the title refers to Jesus' ministry whereas the theology to the situation of the evangelist.

The Shema and John 10

in the introduction of Martyn's third edition of *History and Theology*, Martyn's contribution is that he manages to bring the Gospel of John in dialogue with contemporary Judaism.[81] However, the term "dialogue" used by Moody Smith seems to be insecure. It is more probable that John's Gospel and Jamnian Judaism are responding to the same challenge, that is the destruction of the Temple, rather than engaging each other as will be demonstrated in the following paragraphs. Secondly, it is important to note that although the Gospel of John had a connection with his contemporary Jews, it does not automatically mean that the evangelist would "impose" or "mix up" the experiences of his community with the traditions of Jesus. To say that the evangelist imposes the experiences of his community onto his Gospel—hence it has to be read as a two-level drama[82]—is an anachronism which does not suit the Gospel's genre and the way its reader would read it (pre-critical reading).[83] We will show later that far from imposing his own experiences upon his Gospel, the evangelist was pondering and reflecting on the Jesus tradition and his Jewish heritage, which form his theology, in order to answer to the same challenge faced by Jamnia Judaism (regarding the one God after the destruction of the Temple), when he wrote the Gospel.[84]

To begin with, it is important to note as what Köstenberger has convincingly argued that the destruction of the Temple, the symbol of the oneness God and His people (the *Shema*), is a foreground for the Gospel of John rather than the *Birkhat ha-Minim*.[85] During the Second Temple period, the Temple was deemed as the center for all things.[86] The most important function of the Temple

---

81. Smith, "The Contributon," 1–23.

82. For a review on this, see Hägerland, "John's Gospel," 309–22.

83. Klink, *The Sheep*, 121–47; Young, *Biblical Exegesis*, 139.

84. Cf. Davies, "Reflection," 51. McGrath uses the term apologetic, meaning to defend, to express this idea. See McGrath, *John's Apologetic*.

85. Köstenberger, "Destruction of the Temple," 88, 94; *A Theology*, 422–3.

86. Dunn, *The Partings*, 42–7; Goldenberg, "The Destruction," 192–4. The centrality of the Temple can also be seen as the Jerusalem Temple was regarded as the only "legal" Temple. Köstenberger has rightly asserts that "the erection of the temples at Elephantine (Upper Egypt), Leontopolis (Lower Egypt), and

The Shema as the Framework

is religious in nature. The Temple is the representation of Zion, the place where the true God dwells and His people worship Him.[87] It is also the symbol of the covenant made by God with His people.[88] It is closely connected with the concept of oneness, as noted by Josephus: "one Temple for the one God" (*Ap.* 2.193).[89] However, the Temple was destroyed after AD 70. According to Josephus, "Judaism without the Temple seems to have been unthinkable" (*Ap.* 2.193–8).[90] This was a challenging situation for both the Jews (represented by Jamnian Judaism) and Christians at the time (in this case is the Gospel of John). They were forcefully provoked to think about and to reformulate the concept of oneness which is symbolized by the Temple (the oneness of God and His people).[91] The Jamnian response was to transfer the function of the Temple (the symbol of oneness) to the Synagogue after the former was destroyed.[92] They believe that as God is present in the Temple, he is also present in the Synagogue.[93] To the Jamnian Sages, the oneness God, as the central Synagogue teaching has it, must relate principally to the Torah (as commanded in Deut 6:6–9: the *Shema*). This explains why the Synagogue also functions as the place

---

in Samaria . . . none rivaled the prestige of the Jerusalem sanctuary" (cf. Josephus, *Wars.* 7.2–4, 10). See Köstenberger, "Destruction," 83. In case of the Qumran Community, although they live without the Tempe, their reasons are not whether the Temple is important or not—the Temple is important for them. But, because of the defilement of the Temple by a false priesthood. See: Dunn, *The Partings*, 46; Köstenberger, "Destruction," 83.

87. Dunn, *The Partings*, 44–7; cf. Davies, *The Gospel*, 50–4.

88. Goldenberg, "The Destruction," 196; Wright, *The New Testament*, 226.

89. Sanders, *Judaism*, 50; Dunn, *The Partings*, 46.

90. Thirteen years later, Josephus came to realize that his previous opinion had been mistaken and Judaism could continue even without the Temple. See Köstenberger, "Destruction," 81, 84.

91. Goodman, "The Temple," 463–4. Goodman argues that some Jews are not ready to live without the Temple, so they hope and plan to rebuild the destroyed Temple. It shows how important the Temple to the Jews of the period.

92. Bruce, *New Testament*, 140. Although the Synagogue has been a "temporary" replacement for the Temple, unlike the later, the former can be built more than one.

93. Davies, "Reflection," 48.

The Shema and John 10

for studying Torah and unifying the people of God.[94] They believe that when they obey the Torah and are united as one people, God will restore them.[95] Another interesting observation that can be made regarding Jamnian response to the destruction of the Temple is the restressing of the importance of the *Shema* (which was highly utilized) in this period.[96] This explains why the liturgy in the Synagogue is very similar to the [liturgical] order of the recitation of the *Shema* (see *m. Ber.* 1:14).[97] In doing so, the Sages are using and practicing the *Shema*, in their daily lives (especially in the Synagogue), to maintain the concept of the oneness of God and the oneness of his people after the destruction of the temple.

In the same way, the Gospel of John also responded to the destruction of the temple[98] by focusing on the continuing immanence of the one God and the unity of His people.[99] According to the Gospel of John, the presence of God is not revealed in the temple anymore, but in the presence of Jesus because Jesus is the fulfillment (or even the replacement) of the Temple (see John 2:18–22; 1:14; 1:51; 4:20–24).[100] Jesus represents and reveals (John 1:51)[101] the one God dwelling with His people (John 1:14).[102] This definitely influences how the evangelist of the Fourth Gospel uses

---

94. Davies, "Reflection," 48–9; Köstenberger, "Destruction," 86–7.

95. Köstenberger, "Destruction," 86–7; Goldenberg, "The Destruction," 201–2; Thettayil, *In Spirit*, 243.

96. Segal, *Two Powers*, 138–9; Bruce, *New Testament*, 137.

97. Tan, "Jesus and the *Shema*," 2684; Sanders, *Judaism*, 195–8.

98. Thettayil, *In Spirit*, 241–2.

99. Some first Century Christians interpret the event as a punishment from God for rejecting Jesus. See Davies, "Reflection," 49. Note also that John's response also focuses on the issue of oneness as do the Jews.

100. Hoskins, *Jesus as the Fulfilment*, 104–46. Hoskins argues that the concept of Jesus as the replacement and fulfilment of the Temple is anticipated, even in the Old Testament—as the Temple replaces Bethel and the Tabernacle (Hoskins, *Jesus as the Fulfilment*, 145); cf. Matson, "The Temple Incident," 147–8; Davies, *The Land*, 289; Köstenbeger, *A Theology*, 422–30, 433; Dunn, *The Partings*, 124; Bauckham, *The Testimony*, 263–4.

101. Hoskins, *Jesus as the Fulfilment*, 135.

102. Köstenberger, ""Destruction," 92–3; Cf. Coloe, *God Dwells with Us*, 23–7, 51–55; Davies, *The Land*, 295–6.

and understands the oneness language. To the evangelist, the oneness of God, which is pronounced in the *Shema* and symbolized by the Temple is now revealed in Jesus. A clear depiction of this is also seen in John 10 which will be demonstrated in chapter 3.[103] Another aspect of the fulfillment of the Temple (the place of gathering of the people of God) by Jesus has something to do with the concept of the people of God.[104] Culpepper argues that the criterion to be the children of God (the people of God) is no longer defined by Abraham's filiation, but through accepting Jesus who, representing God, dwells among them (John 1:1–18).[105] The same understanding occurs in John 4, where Jesus redefines who the people of God are.[106] Because Jesus is the fulfillment of the Temple, both Jews and Samaritans need not to worship the one God in the Temple of Jerusalem (destroyed in AD 70) nor the Temple of Mount Gerizim (destroyed in BC 120) (John 4:21).[107] Both of them are to worship the one God in truth and spirit.[108] Despite their differences, there is a fundamental common belief that is held by both Jews and Samaritans, that is, they believe that there is only one God (cf. John 10:16; Ezek 34:22–24)[109]—the creator and revealer, God of Abraham, Isaac and Jacob.[110] Hence, in Jesus both are the people of God. In short, while the Jamnian Judaism replaces the Temple (which is the symbol of oneness) with the Synagogue, the Gospel of John supersedes the Temple with Jesus (who is one with the Father).

103. The fact that John 10 is set in the Festival of Dedication (*Hanukkah*) is no accident. It communicates the importance of the Temple in John's Gospel. In this particular case, the destruction of the temple might be in view, so what is written in John 10 can be seen as a response of the destruction. Cf. Hays, *Echoes of Scripture in the Gospels*, 318

104. Moloney, *The Gospel*, 315–6.

105. Culpepper, "the Pivot," 26–31.

106. Schackenburg, *The Gospel (vol. 1)*, 435–7; Murray, *John*, 61–2.

107. For the Temple of mount Gerizim, see MacDonald, *The Theology*, 330–1.

108. For the relationship between Samaritans and Jews, see Bowman, *The Samaritan Problem*; Hjelm, *The Samaritans*.

109. Bowman, *The Samaritans*, 61–2.

110. See MacDonald, *The Samaritans*, 65–9; Bowman, *The Samaritans*, 30–1.

According to the responses given by both Jamnian Judaism and John's Gospel to the destruction of the Temple, it can be said that both of them are concerned with the concept of oneness symbolized by the Temple. Based on the description above, the two are to maintain the concept of oneness in the *Shema* while responding to the destruction of the Temple. For the benefit of our study, it is important to conclude the importance of the destruction of the Temple event to the oneness theme in the Gospel of John. First of all, the Gospel replaces the Temple with Jesus because Jesus reveals the one God symbolized by the Temple. This explains why he always formulates his oneness concept around the relationship of the Father and Jesus (e.g., John 10; 13; 17; etc.) not the Synagogue as do the Jamian Sages. However, the evangelist does not compromise his monotheistic faith.[111] This explains why the Gospel uses some many terms (e.g., John 7:28; 14:28; 20:21; etc.) to show the dependence of Jesus on God, the Father (will be discussed in chapter three and four).[112] In this regard, the Gospel presents Jesus as the one sent and who acts on behalf of the one God—not a competing god.[113] In other words, the evangelist seems to be defending and explaining more the identity of Jesus in connection with the *Shema* before the Jews after the destruction of the Temple.[114]

Summary

The findings of this chapter can be summarized as follows: 1) The *Shema* is the most important belief of Second Temple Judaism. It does not influence only Jewish beliefs, but also Christian beliefs, including the Gospel of John. In general, the *Shema* has shaped the understanding of God in John's Gospel, particularly through the use of its oneness language. God is understood as the one who creates and reigns over the universe. This one God is also the God

---

111. McGrath, *John's Apologetic*, 233.

112. McGrath, *John's Apologetic*, 77–9.

113. Cf. Baron, "The *Shema* in John's Gospel," 304; Byers, *Ecclesiology and Theosis*, 33.

114. Köstenberger, "Destruction," 87; Dunn, *The Partings*, 209.

who makes a covenant with Israel—His people. The *Shema* also influences the Gospel's oneness language in connection to latter's eschatology and messianism in the way the former influences Second Temple messianism. 2) The *Shema* also plays an important role after the destruction of the Temple. After AD 70, the Jews of the period still recite the *Shema* and use it in the Synagogue, which is a temporary replacement for the Temple. It implies that the one God, as recited in the *Shema*, is still present with them—in the Synagogue. In John's Gospel, the Temple is replaced by the figure of Jesus. As the replacement/fulfillment of the Temple, Jesus redefines the presence of God and who the people of God are (see John 4). It influences the oneness motif of the Gospel because the one God and the one people of God symbolized by the Temple is redefined by the coming of Jesus without compromising the strictness of the oneness of the *Shema*.

3

The *Shema* and John 10 (1)
The echoes and aspects of the *Shema* in John 10

As mentioned in the previous chapter, there are good grounds to believe that the oneness language of John's Gospel has generally been influenced and shaped by the *Shema* in relation to the motifs of the understanding of God, the people of God and the future of the people. The importance of the *Shema* also drives the fourth evangelist to respond to the destruction of the Temple, which also influences the Gospel's oneness language. Hence, the *Shema* may be construed as the foundation of John's theology. In addition to that, the *Shema* has provided a framework for the fourth evangelist to systematically rework and re-present his Jewish belief in light of the Messiah Jesus Christ. This chapter will explore the echoes and the occurrence of the *Shema* framework in John 10.

The Echoes of the *Shema* in John 10

This section will focus only on John 10 and its relation to the *Shema*. However, there are two points that need to be clarified here. The first concerns the structure of John 10. Regarding the original structure, many scholarly proposals have been offered.¹ However, it does not effect this study significantly. Therefore, the structure as found in Nestle Aland 28ed will be used. The second relates to Gerhardsson's warning, which is worth mentioning here. He is right when he says that "when a single element of these general ideas or thoughts (regarding the *Shema*) appears in a New Testament text, it is not self-evident that precisely the *Shema* was in the author's mind when he formulated the words."² This warning has been a concern for some scholars who doubt the echo of the *Shema* can be found in the Gospel of John. Byers has listed some common reservations for this particular concern; the first is that the Gospel of John does not explicitly cite the *Shema* like the Synoptics, and the second has to do with the use of the word "one" where the Septuagint primarily uses the masculine εἷς instead of the neuter ἕν as found in John 10:30 and John 17.³ In light of this warning, it is important to note that the connection between the *Shema* and John 10 should be established on the basis of the available evidence, not on mere conjecture.

Gerhardsson argues that the echoes of the *Shema* in a text can be identified by the occurrence of the two important elements of the *Shema*; these are the introductory word "hear" and the love motif with three qualifications (heart, soul and all resources).⁴ The same attempt, but with a different direction, was made by Erik Waaler in his *The Shema and the First Commandment in First Corinthians*. Waaler argues that "Paul has a particular focus on Deuteronomy in 1 Cor 5:1–10:22."⁵ In addition, he asserts that "it may be argued that the Decalogue and the *Shema* are focal elements in the final version of Deuteronomy, thus it is argued that less verbal agreement and explicit reference is needed for these texts to be echoed."⁶ In connection with 1 Cor 8:6, the echoes of the *Shema*

1. For a brief summary of the proposals, see Murray, *John*, 166.
2. Gerhardsson, *The Shema*, 302.
3. Byers, *Ecclesiology and Theosis*, 137, 140
4. Gerhardsson, *The Shema*, 302–3.
5. Waaler, *The Shema*, 50. Cf. Hays, *Reading Backwards*
6. Waaler, *The Shema*, 50.

The Shema and John 10

can be identified by the presence of the oneness of God motif, the covenant motif, and the people of God motif.[7] In this regard, Waaler is right that the echoes of the *Shema* are not necessarily determined by the verbal similarities and explicit references.

Byers clearly points out that the use of the word "one" (both neuter ἕν in John 10:30 and masculine εἷς like in John 10:16) has made Jesus being accused as blasphemous and punishable by stone.[8] This scene signifies that the use of the word "one" here is not usual and common, but may refer to the one God of the *Shema*.[9] This suggestion is strongly supported by the fact that John 10 alludes to the one shepherd image of Ezek 34 and 37 who is Yahweh, the God of the *Shema*.[10] In addition, the repeated uses of the ἐγώ εἰμί in John 10 (also appear in Ezek 34:15, 20;37:28) also point to the God of the *Shema* in the Old Testament.[11] Similarly, Baron argues that the allusion to the *Shema* in John 10 can be seen through the presence of hearing, oneness, love, and life motifs.[12]

Furthermore, it is important to know the form of the *Shema* in this period. As stated by Tan Kim Huat, it is widely accepted that the *Shema* as known and recited today has undergone the following stages: "(i) the recitation of Deut. 6:4; (ii) the reading of Deut. 6:4–9; (iii) the reading of Deut. 6:4–9; 11.13–21; Num. 15:37–41; and (iv) the additions of the benedictions."[13] It is quite probable that the Gospel of John is composed in the period in which stages iii and iv are taking place. However, what really is important for this study is stage iii. The recitation of Deut 6:4–9; 11:13–21 and Num 15:37–41, instead of Deut 6:4–9 only shows not only that the

---

7. Waaler, *The Shema*, 114; cf. Wright, *The Climax*, 120–36.

8. Byers, *Ecclesiology and Theosis*, 136

9. Baron sees the act of accusing Jesus making himself God and the attempt to stone him can be read in light of Deut 6:4, where Jesus' statement in John 10:30 may refer to the oneness language of Deut 6:4–5. See Baron, "The *Shema* and the Gospel of John," 333

10. Byers, *Ecclesiology and Theosis*, 137

11. Byers, *Ecclesiology and Theosis*, 138–9

12. Baron, "The *Shema* and the Gospel of John," 334–59

13. Tan, "Jesus and the *Shema*," 2682.

The Shema and John 10 (1)

Shema is repeatedly and continuously stressed, but also the core of the *Shema* has undergone development over the years. The core motifs found in those three passages can be summarized as follows: 1) The relational (covenantal) oneness motif—of God and His people. God is depicted as the one who reveals himself as the only God (e.g., Deut 6:4; Num 15:41).[14] He is also the one who makes a covenantal relationship with his people (Deut 6:6; Num 15:38, 41) and their descendants (e.g., Deut 6:7-9; 11:19-21; Num 15:38; cf. Deut 11:9). This covenantal relationship is also revealed in the context of obeying the law (Deut 11:13; Num 15:39-40) followed by its consequences (Deut 11:14-17). 2) The love motif—of God and his people. Love is the most obvious trait of the *Shema* as observed by scholars.[15] In the *Shema*, the love for the one God is depicted as the people's response to the covenant made between them and their God (Deut 6:5; 11:13, 18). It is also presented as a command from God (Deut 6:6; 11:13; Num 15: 39). 3) The deliverance motif. The *Shema* first appeared in the context of the deliverance of Israel from Egypt. God's people remember and celebrate the greatness of their God who has brought them out of slavery (Num 15:41; cf. Deut 6:12; 11:3-7). In the *Shema*, God's people are also reminded about the promise made by their God—to bring them to Zion (cf. Deut 6:3, 10-11; 11:9-12). This promise, then becomes the people's greatest hope during the Second Temple period. 4) The last but not least is the importance of the hearing motif (Deut 6:4).[16] In those three passages (Deut 6:4; cf. Deut 11:13; Num 15:37), the hearing aspect plays an important role for indicating the relationship of the one God with His people. That is why the word "hear" or *Shema* is chosen to be the proper noun for the Jewish core belief.

Those core motifs are also found or echoed in John 10.[17] John 10 does not present the oneness motif as a numeral oneness,

---

14. See Appold, *The Oneness Motif*, 12-3.
15. Cf. Varghese, *The Imagery*, 316.
16. Gerhadsson, *The Shema*, 302; cf. Baron, "The Shema in John's Gospel," 311-4, 316, 334-5
17. Söding, "Ich und der Vater," 177-99; Cf. Thompson, "Every Picture,"

The Shema and John 10

but a relational oneness as does the *Shema*. The relational oneness is shown by the relationship of Jesus and the Father (John 10:15, 30, 38).[18] This oneness is the foundation for the oneness of the one God and His people—depicted as one Shepherd and one folk (John 10:16).[19] This relationship is so strong that no one can separate it (John 10:28–29).[20] It is obviously an echo of the covenantal relationship in the Old Testament. The love motif which defines the relationship of the one God and his people is also clearly seen in John 10. The evangelist makes it clear that love actually originated from God, as shown in the love between Jesus and the Father (John 10:17). In addition, the loving relationship of the one God with his people is seen in the act of salvation performed by Jesus (John 10:11, 15, 17–18).[21] This marks the overlapping or connection between the love motif and the deliverance motif in the *Shema*. Besides the salvation/deliverance idea which has taken place by the act of Jesus (it is also known as realized eschatology), John 10 also presents another dimension of the deliverance motif—that is Zion. In John 10:28, 10, 9, the promise of Zion in the *Shema* is now depicted as eternal life.[22] In addition, as carefully noted by Richard Hays, the allusion to Ezek 34 in John 10 is very clearly and important. The importance of the allusion is that the one God of the *Shema* has been made known (incarnate) in the person of Jesus

---

265, 267–8; Waaler, *The Shema*, 41. Based on the findings of the previous section, it is evident that the *Shema* is available to the Gospel of John and its audience. In this regard, the *Shema* is understood as both an intertextual echo and a dialogical intertextuality—to use Steve Moyise's terms. See Moyise, "Intertextuality," 18–32.

18. Schnackenburg, *John*, 308; Baron, "The *Shema* in John's Gospel," 335–54. This idea that the oneness language in John 10:30 probably was influenced by the *Shema* had firstly been pointed out by Barret in 1947, see Baron, "The *Shema* in John's Gospel," 3, 286–8; Byers, *Ecclesiology and Theosis*, 108.

19. Moloney, *John*, 305; Schnackenburg, *John*, 299, 308; cf. Murray, *John*, 171.

20. Haechen, *John*, 50.

21. Frey, "Love-Relations," 189; cf. Thompson, "Every Picture," 271–3.

22. Moloney, *John*, 315; Baron, "The *Shema* in John's Gospel," 357–9

The Shema and John 10 (1)

whom will bring deliverance to His people.[23] Another echo of the *Shema* that can be found in John 10 is the motif of hearing and doing.[24] John 10 carefully shows that the relationship between the one God and His people is determined by the hearing and doing motif, where those who belong to Him will hear and do His command (John 10:3-5, 16, 27).[25]

The Different Aspects of the *Shema* Framework in John 10

Any use of the Old Testament (e.g., quotations, allusions, echoes, etc.) or other traditions in the New Testament (or other writings) involve a process of introducing a new context to pre-formed materials.[26] This is true also for the *Shema* in John 10. As a comparison, the *Shema* is also put in a new context by the Synoptic Gospels, e.g., the *Shema* in the temptation of Jesus by Satan (Matt 4:1-11; Luke 4:1-13).[27] Similarly, the *Shema* in John 10 is put into the context of the imagery of the Shepherd and the door which contains echoes of Ezek 34 (and Pss 23; 94; Num 27; etc.)[28] and Ps 118.[29] Sociologically speaking, the same *Shema* is put into the context of conflict over the identity of Jesus (John 10:19-39).[30] In these two new contexts—both textual and social—the *Shema* is uniquely understood and used. There are several aspects at-

---

23. Hays, *Echoes of Scripture in the Gospels*, 318-20
24. Baron, "The *Shema* in John's Gospel," 334-5
25. Barrett, *John*, 261.
26. See Stamps, "The Use," 13-4.
27. Gerhadsson, *The Shema*, 304-6. In this case, Gerhadsson argues that the *Shema* is put into an apologetic situation. The *Shema* does carry the meaning of Deut. 6, but it is also understood differently in this instance—that is the *Shema* and the tempting.
28. Zimmermann, "Jesus im Bild Gottes," 101-11; Bultmann, *The Gospel of John*, 364-7; Smith, *John*, 205; Scnackenburg, *John*, 295; Moloney, *John*, 301; Köstenberger, *A Theology of John's*, 308-9.
29. Brunson, *Psalm 118*, Ch. 9-10.
30. Ensor, *Jesus*, 232-8.

The Shema and John 10

tached to it. These aspects are: 1) The inclusion of Jesus in the understanding of the oneness of God. As shown in the previous chapter, monotheism in Second Temple Judaism is not understood numerically, but relationally.[31] This understanding also appears in John 10. In John 10, the relationship between Jesus and the Father is a foundation for the relationship of the one God and His people (John 10:30, 38).[32] We will call this aspect the theological aspect, which will be discussed later. 2) The redefined concept of the covenant and election. The people of God are also not only restricted to the physical heirs of Abraham, but to the relationship one has with the one God (John 10:16),[33] that is he who hears and does what the one God has commanded (John 10:3–5, 16, 27). It means the concepts of covenant and election are redefined in a new way. The one God performs a new deliverance (John 10:9–10, 15–18, 28), which is connected with what He did in the past (Deut 6; 11; Num 15). Through this deliverance, the people will be constituted. This aspect will be called the ecclesiological aspect. 3) The hope of the return of Yahweh to Zion is incorporated to the eschatology of the Gospel. Significantly, the return of Yahweh to Zion is also connected the deliverance of His people. In John 10, the deliverance is defined and done by the work of Jesus on behalf of the one God (John 10:18, 36–38). Jesus is the eschatological Messiah, who will deliver His people. However, His coming is not the conclusion of the promise, but the start of the final consummation. This understanding of eschatology is also widely known as the "already-but-not-yet concept."

---

31. Byers, *Ecclesiology and Theosis*, 137; Baron, "The *Shema* in John's Gospel," 349–50.

32. Cf. Murray, *John*, 171.

33. Cf. Bernard, *St. John Vol. 2*, 362; Baron, "The *Shema* in John's Gospel," 334–5.

4

The *Shema* and John 10 (2)

The *Shema* Framework and John 10

As PREVIOUSLY MENTIONED, THE *Shema* framework proposed in this book consists of three different aspects; the theological, ecclesiological, and eschatological aspects. This chapter will try to read the oneness language in John 10 using that proposed framework.

The Theological Aspect: Christological Monotheism.

Christology is the central theme of John's Gospel. Many approaches have been employed for understanding it, and they may be grouped into four categories, as proposed by Paul N. Anderson: 1) Text-centered approaches, which focus on the Christological titles, motifs, and central structures in John's Gospel; 2) Theological-Christological approaches, which concentrate on the theological issues of the Christology of the Gospel; 3) Literary-Christological approaches, which are concerned mainly with the literary aspects of the Christology of the Gospel; and 4) Historical-Christological approaches, which center on the historical elements of the Christology in the Gospel.¹ All these approaches are helpful, but on their own they are also too narrow, because they tackle John's Christology, as it stands, independently from its theology.² As stated earlier, the inclusion of Jesus into the Gospel's theology is the key to understanding its Christology. However, Johannine scholars tend to treat the concept of God in the Gospel of John as though it is subjugated to its Christology.³ It is evident that Christology is a major theme in the Gospel. However, it is mistaken to subjugate John's understanding of God (hereafter: theology) to it. What is presented in John is rather that its Christology seems to be subjugated to its theology, although Jesus is also presented as one with the Father (John 10:30).⁴ The presentation of Jesus in the Gospel of John always reminds the readers that Jesus is dependent on God for all his actions. Although Jesus is doing things that can only be done by God alone (e.g., raising the dead, see John 11), he does it on behalf of God, he is not another god. The following paragraphs will be dealing with this issue.

T. E. Pollard is right when he argues that "the Gospel of St John is pre-eminently the Gospel of 'the Father (theology) and the Son (Christology).'"⁵ In other words, in order to understand John's Christology, one has to deal with the relationship between the Father and the Son. This christological model is called and known as christological monotheism.⁶ Although christological

1. Anderson, *The Christology*, 17–31.

2. An exception is the treatment of the issue in the Theological-Christological Approaches group. However, this approach tends to see Jesus' subordination contradicts His equality to the Father (Anderson, *The Christology*, 24–5). It is because the approach misapplies categories for understanding the relationship of Jesus and the Father.

3. See how majority scholars tend to approach John's theology and end up subjugating it to John's Christology: Sadananda, *The Johannine*.

4. Haenchen, *John 2*, 50.

5. Pollard, *Johannine Christology*, 15–6.

6. In recent years, there are many christological model offered by scholars to approach the Christology of the Fourth Gospel and the New Testament (e.g., Incarnational Christology, Adoption Christology, Apologetic Christology, etc.). The term christological monotheism here is used in connection with the idea of the oneness relationship of Jesus and the Father (monotheism).

The Shema and John 10 (2)

monotheism is clearly reflected in the relationship between Jesus and the Father, it does not mean that the relationship can be easily explained and understood. In John 10, Jesus is portrayed as equal[7] (John 10:30, 38) and yet subordinate to the Father (John 10:18, 27, 36–7). Commenting on this, Barrett suggests that the relationship carries both an ontological and a moral sense for John's Gospel.[8] The suggestion is interesting, but yet questionable. It seems that Barrett is using the fourth century's philosophical category, such as ontology, in his suggestion. Knowing that the Gospel's theology is heavily influenced by the Jewish worldview (rather than Hellenistic philosophy), it appears implausible that the evangelist would understand the relationship ontologically.[9] On the contrary, Pollard offers a new set of categories for understanding the relationship; These are: (1) moral likeness;[10] and (2) essential identity.[11] The latter is may be deemed adequate[12] in speaking of the oneness

---

7. Sadananda tries to differentiate the word "equal" and "one" in the sense that the word ἕν contains the meaning of equal in power, role, and status than the oneness (see Sadananda, *The Johannine*, 120). His suggestion is interesting, but it is not supported by any strong evidence. To me, there is no difference in saying that "Jesus is equal to the Father in their status" from "Jesus is in the same status with the Father." Thus, such differentiation seems to be redundant here. So, this section will use the term interchangeably.

8. Barrett, *John*, 60; cf. Pollard, *Johannine*, 17.

9. Cf. Pollard, *Johannine*, 17. The Jews do not understand their God philosophically, but rather practically and relationally through their experiences with Him (cf. Chapter 2).

10. This term is understood in the way that Jesus morally does what the Father does (e.g. In 10:14–15 God knows His own, so does Jesus)

11. Pollard, *Johannine*, 17. This suggestion reflects Pollard's attempt to read John's Gospel in the first century setting in contrast to the anachronistic reading of John.

12. To some, e.g. Dunn, *Did the First Christians*, ch. 3, the idea of identity may seem to be odd or even anachronistic. However, the idea of identity, both of God and His people, was present in the Second Temple period and Jamnian Judaism. The Second Temple sects, e.g. Qumran, Pharisees, Zealots, etc., defined their own identity on the basis of their understanding of God's identity—Yahweh. The same is true for the Sages of the Jamnia who struggled about God's and their identity in the light of the destruction of Jerusalem, or the Temple in particular. In short, the idea of social or religious identity is not odd nor anachronistic in the period. In case of John 10, the idea of identity

of Jesus with the Father, while the former is still too narrow[13] for describing the subordination of Jesus to the Father, as will be demonstrated by the following close reading of John 10.

The most striking verse that speaks of the oneness of Jesus with the Father is 10:30: ἐγὼ καὶ ὁ πατὴρ ἕν ἐσμεν (see also John 5:18; 19:7).[14] This verse has long read through the lens of the fourth century Christological debates.[15] In modern scholarship, the word ἕν has been taken to prove the oneness "of essence between the Father and Son", while the word ἐσμεν indicates "the difference of persons."[16] Bauckham argues that the verse must be read in its own context. He believes that the word "one" (ἕν) is an echo of the *Shema* (see chapter 2).[17] At the same time, however, he is also aware that the allusion or echo to the *Shema* in the New Testament is always in the masculine (εἷς, e.g., Rom 3:30; Gal 3:20; Jas 2:19), instead of the neuter (ἕν). He argues that "this is a necessary adaptation of language, (since) Jesus is not saying that he and the Father are a single person (εἷς)[18], but that together they are

---

is clearly stated through the use of particular language and expressions (e.g. 10:1–2 use the language and expression which are functioned to clarify the identity of the true Shepherd; 10:7, 9, 11, 14 use the ἐγώ εἰμι language to define the identity of Jesus; 10:16, 26 indicate the identity of Jesus' followers). Coloe even argues that the setting of the narrative itself indicates the idea of the revealing of the identity of Jesus. See Coloe, *God Dwells*, 146–7. This suggestion is in line with the main question asked by the first century Jews that is who God is (identity), not what God is (essence).

13. This section does not intend to deny the fact that Jesus morally does what the Father does or intends to do. However, the term "moral likeness" itself seems to be insufficient for explaining what Jesus does in connection with His subordination to the Father. "Moral likeness" does not require subordination language to operate (e.g., 1 Cor. 4:16, 11:1). The category argued in this section is, I suggest, the revelational oneness. As will be explained next, the revelational oneness explains both Jesus' works as from and dependent on the Father.

14. Cf. Forestell, *The Word*, 39.

15. Bernard, *John*, 365.

16. Bernard, *John*, 365.

17. Bauckham, *The Testimony*, 250; "Biblical Theology," 227; *Jesus and the God*, 104; Köstenberger, *A Theology*, 374; *John*, 312.

18. Cf. Morris, *The Gospel*, 465.

(ἐσμεν) one God."[19] His argument is substantiated by the use of the same construction ("singular-neuter" and "plural-masculine") in 1 Cor 3:8 and John 17:22. 1 Cor 3:8 reads ὁ φυτεύων δὲ καὶ ὁ ποτίζων ἕν (singular-neuter) εἰσιν (plural-masculine). There, Paul is asserting that both the one planting and the one watering are (εἰσιν) not the same (one) person(s), but they belong to the same category of identity (ἕν)—that is the workers of God (see 1 Cor 3:9).[20] The same is true for John 17.22 which reads ὦσιν (plural-masculine) ἕν (singular-neuter) καθὼς[21] ἡμεῖς (plural-masculine) ἕν (singular-neuter). In John 17:22, Jesus does not mean or hope that the disciples will become one person, but they will be a part of a community—the same category (God's people), just as Jesus and the Father are in the same category (God).[22] In the light of this, what Bauckham means by "a necessary adaptation of language" in John 10:30 can be understood as indicating that Jesus and the Father are not the same person(s) (ἕν), but they belong to the same category of identity—that is the divine identity (God).[23] Using Byers's words, this verse shows that "the evangelist takes considerable pains in deftly coordinating Jesus with God in such a way that they share the divine identity without one absorbing into

19. Bauckham, *The Testimony*, 251; "Biblical Theology," 227; *Jesus and the God*, 104; cf. Pollard, *Johannine*, 17–8.

20. Baron also consults 1 Cor. 3:8 to investigate the use of ἕν instead of εἷς in this context, but uses the term "entity" to describe the importance of ἕν in John 10:30. Here, I use the term "the same category of identity" (that is, to use the term coined by Bauckham, the divine identity) in order to specify the sameness (oneness) of Jesus and the Father. See Baron, "The *Shema* in John's Gospel," 349–50.

21. Καθώς plays a significant role here as in John 10:16 that is to stress that the foundation of the oneness of God's people is the oneness of Jesus and the Father.

22. Byers, *Ecclesiology and Theosis*, 196

23. Bauckham, *Jesus and the God*, 105. This is no strange idea to the New Testament writings, since it also appears elsewhere in the New Testament; Carson and Köstenberger argue that the oneness must be more than the oneness of wills or actions. It indicates the oneness of identity, although they think it is not absolute. See Carson, *John*, 392, 395; Köstenberger, *John*, 311, 312; Köstenberger and Swain, *Father, Son and Spirit*, 111–2; cf. Byers, *Ecclesiology and Theosis*, 123, 140

The Shema and John 10

the other."[24] In addition, 1 Cor 3:8; John 17:22 and 10:30 seem to have common expressions, though implicit. All of them suggest that those who belong to the same category of identity might have the (one) same purpose or goal. For 1 Cor 3:8, the same purpose Paul and Apollos have is seen in 3:6-7, that is the growth of God's people. For John 17:22, the purpose is reciprocally stated, that is to love and to make God known through the one he has sent (John 17:21, 23).[25] In John 10, Jesus and the Father are also depicted as having the same purpose (as Jesus does the works of the Father), that is to save, gather, give eternal life, and lead the people (the sheep) (John 10:9-11, 14-18, 27-29, 37-38).

In connection with 10.38: ἐν ἐμοὶ ὁ πατὴρ κἀγὼ ἐν τῷ πατρί, Scholtissek argues that "Diese Einheit von Vater und Sohn ist eine personale Beziehung Wirk lichkeit, die bei aller Konformität und wesensmäßigen Zugehörigkeit auch eine bleibende Unterschiedenheit kennt."[26] He insists that the reciprocal indwelling (personal relationship: *eine personale Beziehung*) of Jesus and the Father (ἐν ἐμοὶ ... ἐν τῷ πατρί) has to be understood in terms of membership of the same category (*Zugehörigkeit*) in which the identity of each member is distinct from each other (*Unterschiedenheit*).[27] The inclusion of Jesus in the category of divine identity is further expressed by the use of ἐγώ εἰμι (both the absolute and predicative form) phrase throughout chapter 10 (John 10:7, 9, 11, 14; cf. John 10:30, 36) which is an echo of Exod

---

24. Byers, *Ecclesiology and Theosis*, 122

25. Carson, *John*, 569.

26. Scholtissek, "Ich und der Vater," 339.

27. Cf. Bauckham, *The Testimony*, 251; Köstenberger, *A Theology*, 360; In their commentary on John, Jey J. Kanagaraj and Ian S. Kemp argue that "biblical thought person stands for relationships, not for individual as is Western thought... the Father and Son are two identities." Up to this point, they are right. However, they seem to be inconsistent when talking about the nature of the oneness of Jesus and the Father. Although they have already identified that the oneness include the notion of relationship which makes the oneness falls into the divine identity criterion, they suggest that the oneness is the oneness of Godhead (it is not clear what they mean by Godhead. It can either mean the divine identity [who God is] or essence [what God is]) and of will. See Kanagaraj and Kemp, *The Gospel*, 258.

The Shema and John 10 (2)

3:24 (see Isa 43:25; 45:19 [LXX]) a locus classicus for understanding the revelation of God's identity.[28] Here, by introducing himself as God did in the Old Testament, Jesus is not only revealing God, but also disclosing his identity which is in the same category with God.[29] This explanation is in line with John 10:33, 39, where Jesus is not accused of considering himself a second or competing god, but making Himself (ποιεῖς σεαυτὸν) in the same category with God (John 10:36: God's Son) (cf. John 5:18; 19.7; Lev 24:16; *m. Sa.* 7:4).[30] Morris, quoting Hoskyns, argues that "the Jews would not presumably have treated as blasphemy, the idea that a man could regulate his words and actions according to the will of God."[31] In other words, Jesus' unity with the Father is more than the unity of will, but something that can be considered as blasphemy—that is, including oneself in the category of divine identity.[32]

John 10:38 also plays a significant role for understanding the subordination of Jesus to the Father. As observed by Cowan, the subordination language is clearly used in John's Gospel, including John 10. There are at least three types of language used in describing this; These are: 1) The sending language used in John's Gospel; 2) The language of Jesus' dependence on the Father; and 3) The

28. Bauckham, *The Testimony*, 247–8; cf. Harris, *Prologue and Gospel*, 147–9. Although she is not sure about the background of the "I am the Good Shepherd" saying (because she relies too much on Bultmann and Knox), Elizabeth Harris argues that the use of predicate καλός after the ἐγώ εἰμι (10:11, 14) has something to do with Jesus' oneness with the Father and His revelatory works.

29. Cf. Moody, *John*, 212.

30. Moody, *John*, 465; Bauckham, *The Testimony*, 251; von Wahlde, *The Gospel*, 473–4; Hurtado, "Pre-70 CE Jewish Opposition," 36–7.

31. Morris, *John*, 465

32. Bernard, *John*, 367. In this regard, Jesus' response is interesting and yet enigmatic, that He alludes to Psalm 82.6. It raises many interpretations (see Brown, *John Vol. 1*, 408–410; Carson, *John*, 397–400; Köstenberger, *John* 314–15). What important is that Jesus is contrasting Himself with god(s) who are fallen (Ps 82:7) because He is one with the Father. In other words, if the Jews had no problem with calling any man a god (most likely refers to Israel—God's firstborn son), there will be no problem accepting Jesus' claim. Cf. McGrath, *John's Apologetic*, 121–4, 130; Neyrey, *The Gospel*, 178–9; De Jonge, "Monotheism and Christology," 234.

use of the phrase "the Father and Son" in describing the relationship of the two[33] According to Borgen, subordination language, as found in John 10, is used to communicate the idea of agency. As the agent of God, Jesus reveals the Father who is one [in the same category] with Him.[34] In other words, the subordination language does not contradict the oneness language, but [they both] rather complement each other. In this regard, Scholtissek is right when he contends that the subordination will not destroy "die Einheit und Einigkeit Gottes," because the language used is meant and has to be understood as revelational (*Offenbarung*) oneness of Jesus and the Father.[35] In John 10:38, Jesus is revealing (*offenbarend*) the Father through his works (John 10:25, 32, 37–8a; cf. John 5:23; 12:44–45; 13:20; 15:23).[36] This revealing activity is also clearly expressed in Jesus' response to the accusation thrown by the Jews (John 10:36). In John 10:36, Jesus is confirming that He is God's son which can be understood as God's agent/messiah whose aim is to reveal God as understood by the Old Testament and Second Temple Judaism.[37] The same occurs in John 10:15: καθὼς[38] γινώσκει με ὁ πατὴρ κἀγὼ γινώσκω τὸν πατέρα, καὶ τὴν ψυχήν μου τίθημι ὑπὲρ τῶν προβάτων.[39] John 10:15 reveals 1) Jesus'

33. Cowan, "The Father and Son," 115-35; cf. Loader, *The Christology*, 163-4; cf. Olsson, "Deus Semper Maior?," 350, 373.

34. Borgen, "God's Agent," 68-9.

35. Scholtissek, "Ich und der Vater," 339; Forestell, *The Word*, 37-8; James Montgomery Boice argues that the subornation language in John's Gospel (e.g. 3.11; 7.16, 17; 10.37, 38) has a strong connection with Jesus' revelatory role in revealing the Father. See Boice, *Witness and Revelation*, 55; cf. Olsson, "Deus Semper Maior?," 167.

36. Ensor, *Jesus*, 234-8; cf. Rae, "The Testimony," 297-8; Köstenberger, *A Theology*, 385; cf. Anderson, *The Christology*, 267; cf. Pollard, *Johannine*, 21; Forestell, *The Word*, 56; Mlakuzhyil, *The Christocentric*, 277.

37. Cf. McGrath, *John's Apologetic*, 126-7.

38. The use of καθώς in this context is very important. It shows that the foundation of Jesus' relationship in 10:14 (γινώσκω τὰ ἐμὰ καὶ γινώσκουσίν με τὰ ἐμά) is His relationship with the Father (10:15). This relationship of Jesus and the Father is also the reason for Jesus' act in 10:15b (τὴν ψυχήν μου τίθημι).

39. There are two possible renderings for this verse; these are: (1) As the Father knoweth me, so I know the Father. (2) (10:14: I know mine, and mine

The Shema and John 10 (2)

reciprocal relationship with the Father (γινώσκει ... γινώσκω); and 2) Jesus' act of giving His life (τὴν ψυχήν μου τίθημι). The purpose is inevitably soteriological, but the foundation of the act itself is the relational and revelational oneness Jesus has with the Father.[40] In other words, this soteriological purpose shows that Jesus and the Father have the same (one) purpose or goal that is to save the people through Jesus' life-giving action (cf. 10:37: Jesus does the Father's works). This affirms that the same purpose in John 10, has to be understood as an expression of relational and revelational oneness, rather than the foundation of the unity itself. The upshot of all this is that Pollard's category of moral likeness is too narrow in capturing this reality. Jesus acts not only as the Father does, but he also reveals the Father through his words, deeds, and purpose of coming (cf. John 14:10–11).[41]

To sum up, Köstenberger's words are worth noting here: "in its portrayal of Jesus as distinct from God and yet intrinsic to his identity, John's Gospel does not compromise Jewish monotheism... Jesus was not a second god, that is, a divine entity apart from the one and only God revealed in Scripture as the Creator and Ruler of all things."[42] In this regard, the *Shema* helps us to understand that the Christology of the Fourth Gospel is neither simply subordinationism nor fourth century's Trinitarianism, but christological monotheism—Jesus is in the same category with the Father and revealing the Father at the same time. The *Shema* framework—relational and revelational oneness—offers a new category for understanding the Christology of the Fourth Gospel, that is, Jesus' inclusion in the divine identity of God and Jesus' subordination as the way to revealing His Father.

---

know me,) even (καθώς) as the Father knoweth me, and I know the Father. The best rendering is the latter for it explains the connection of verse 14 and 15 (and 17; and comparable to 6:57; 17:21). See Bernard, *John*, 360; cf. de Jonge, *Christology*, 147.

40. Bernard, *John*, 360; Harris, *Prologue*, 148–9.

41. In this regard, Bultmann is right when he argues that the core of John's Gospel is the revelation of God to the world. See Bultmann, *Theology of the New Testament Vol. 2*.

42. Köstenberger, *A Theology*, 360.

The Shema and John 10

The Ecclesiological Aspect: The People of God (Re)-united.[43]

The second important aspect of the *Shema* in John 10 is the oneness of the people of God—the people of the covenant.[44] The Jewish understanding of this aspect—the oneness of the people, Temple, and Torah—is determined by the oneness of God (see Philo, *Spec.* 1.52; 4.159; *Virt.* 35; Josephus, *Ant.* 5.111).[45] The people of God are the elect ones, and their oneness is based on the covenant they have with their God (Gen 12; Deut 27-30; Jub 12:19-20).[46] The same is true for John's Gospel, as can be seen in the use of the two images—the door (θύρα) and the good shepherd (ποιμήν)—in John 10. The door image (10:1-2, 7, 9) is an allusion to Psalm 118 (117 in LXX) as can be seen in the following arguments:[47]

John 10:7b, 9	Psalm 117:19-20 (LXX)	Ps. 118:19-20 (MT)
7b ἀμὴν ἀμὴν λέγω ὑμῖν ὅτι ἐγώ εἰμι <u>ἡ θύρα</u> τῶν προβάτων.	¹⁹ ἀνοίξατέ μοι <u>πύλας</u> δικαιοσύνης <u>εἰσελθὼν</u> ἐν αὐταῖς ἐξομολογήσομαι τῷ κυρίῳ	¹⁹ פִּתְחוּ־לִי שַׁעֲרֵי־צֶדֶק אָבֹא־בָם אוֹדֶה יָהּ׃
⁹ ἐγώ εἰμι <u>ἡ θύρα</u>· δι' ἐμοῦ ἐάν τις <u>εἰσέλθῃ</u> σωθήσεται καὶ <u>εἰσελεύσεται</u> καὶ ἐξελεύσεται καὶ νομὴν εὑρήσει.	²⁰ αὕτη <u>ἡ πύλη</u> τοῦ κυρίου δίκαιοι <u>εἰσελεύσονται</u> ἐν αὐτῇ	²⁰ זֶה־הַשַּׁעַר לַיהוָה צַדִּיקִים יָבֹאוּ בוֹ׃

---

43. Here, ecclesiology or ecclesiological aspect will be understood as the concept of the unity and the identity of the people of God and its connection with the *Shema*, rather than the doctrine of the Church with its ramification, e.g., baptism, sacrament, mission, etc. See Ferreira, *Johannine Ecclesiology*, 45.

44. Cf. 2 Bar 48:23-24; Josephus, *Ant.* 4.201; *C. Ap.* 2.193.

45. Bauckham, *The Testimony*, 251.

46. Pryor, *John*, 157-8.

47. Brunson, *Psalm 118*, 325-44; Similarly, Köstenberger argues that the Psalm is used in John 10 as it is used in John 12.13 (see Köstenberger, *John*, 302-3.); Brown, *John I-XII*, 394-5; Beasly-Murray, *John*, 169. The basis for the oneness of the people of God is further describe in chapter 17 of the Gospel. There, the oneness of the people of God (represent by the oneness of the disciples) is an "imitation" of the oneness Jesus has with the Father.

The Shema and John 10 (2)

As mentioned by Brunson, the main difficulty for arguing that ἡ θύρα in John 10:7, 9 is an allusion to Ps 117:19–20 (LXX), is that the LXX version of the Psalm has ἡ πύλη instead of ἡ θύρα.[48] However, the connection between John 10 and Psalm 117 (LXX) can still be made by looking at the verb εἰσέρχομαι which is used twice by both passages. Regarding the different word used for the door in John (ἡ θύρα) and in the LXX version of the Psalm (ἡ πύλη), Brunson argues: 1) The Hebrew שַׁעֲרֵי is translated by both πύλη and θύρα (see Ezek 46:12 [LXX] uses both πύλη and θύρα to translate שַׁעֲרֵי); 2) The use of both nouns in the NT suggests that they are sometimes interchangeable, especially when applied to the temple gate (see Acts 3:2; 21:30 [πύλη] and Acts 3:10 [θύρα]); 3) The NT writers are more familiar with θύρα than πύλη as the former appears four times as often as the latter; and interestingly the word πύλη does not appear in John's Gospel at all; and finally, 4) The word θύρα has a wider semantic range than πύλη. Thus, the fourth evangelist might prefer to use the former in order to refer to the door in John 10 as both for the sheepfold (John 10:1, 2) and for himself (John 10:7, 9). This means the fourth evangelist could have used either the LXX or the Hebrew version of the Psalm for the sake of his argument.[49] In addition, the background and literary context of both passages seem to be very similar in that there are at least three figures mentioned: 1) The savior; 2) The suffering people; and 3) The oppressors. The occasions of the two passages also look very similar in that the suffering or oppressed are waiting for the deliverance.[50] These arguments presented by Brunson seem to pass the seven criteria given by Hays in order to identify an echo/allusion in the New Testament.[51]

48. Brunson, *Psalm 118*, 328.

49. Brunson, *Psalm 118*, 328–9.

50. Brunson, *Psalm 118*, 330–4.

51. The seven criteria are: 1) Availability [Brunson's book has proved that Psalm 118 is available to the Gospel of John]; 2) Volume [the use of the verb εἰσέρχομαι twice and the same pattern]; 3) Recurrence [cf. John 8.56, 10.24–25]; 4) Thematic coherence [the two passages have a common theme of deliverance]; 5) Historical plausibility [the figure of Jesus seen as the fulfillment of what had been written in Psalm 118]; 6) History of interpretation

The Shema and John 10

Brunson argues that there are three functions of the allusion in this context: 1) To establish the exclusivity of Jesus' mediatorial role and the exclusivity of the new community; 2) To include those who enter through the door; and 3) To declare the Christological role of Jesus.[52] These three points correspond with John 10:8-10, in which, on the one hand, the exclusiveness of the new community is indicated by the unresponsiveness of the sheep toward the voice of the thieves (κλέπται) and robbers (λῃσταί), but the positive response toward Jesus' voice (John 10:16). On the other hand, the inclusiveness of the community is depicted through the welcoming of whoever (ἐάν + τίς) enters through the door (John 10:16). There are two implications arising from this. 1) The coming of Jesus defines who the true shepherd is (see John 10:10). This refers to the revelational oneness Jesus has with the Father, where Jesus is the only one capable of revealing the true shepherd from the false;[53] and 2) The voice of Jesus defines who the sheep are (John 10:8-9).[54] It indicates the concept of election and covenant of God with his people (see chapter 2). In light of John 10:25-6 (cf. John 10:27), the elect are they who hear, acknowledge and follow the voice of Jesus. Interestingly the election and covenant concept are resounded with an invitation or calling nuance (those who are elected and living in the covenant are those who hear and accept the calling). The identity of the true sheep depends on their response to the calling; if they accept, they will be counted as the true Sheep. In John 10:9-10 the privilege of being God's people is

---

[there are many other scholars who think that John 10.7, 9 is an allusion of Psalm 118.19-20. Some of them are Velasco, "Puerta," 39-50; Simonis, *Die Hirtenrede*, 251-3]; 7) Satisfaction [the readers of the Gospel of John might find this allusion satisfactory as it is contextualized into the readers' context, cf. Brunson, *Psalm 118*, 330-4]. Hays, *Echoes of the Scripture in the Letters of Paul*, 29-33.

52. Brunson, *Psalm 118*, 340-5.

53. In connection with the second image—the Shepherd, which is an allusion to Ezek. 34—the reference to the false shepherd refers to the ruler of Israel (cf. Ezek. 34:2-4). In John's context, it could possibly refer to the Pharisees and their associates (cf. John 9). See: Brown, *John Vol. I-XII*, 393-4, 398; Köstenberger, *John*, 303; cf. Pryor, *John*, 167-73.

54. Brunson, *Psalm 118*, 349.

The Shema and John 10 (2)

stated—they "will be saved, and will come in and go out and find pasture" (John 10:9)[55] and "they may have life, and have it abundantly" (John 10:10; cf. John 10:28).[56] In other words, God's people are, on the one hand exclusive in terms of their relationship with their God, but, on the other, they are inclusive because the people are whoever enters through the door, which is Jesus. This point will be further discussed in the next section (John 10:16).

The second image, the shepherd image in John 10:11, 14, and 16, is obviously an allusion to the Old Testament image of God or his messiah (see Ezek 34; Ps 23, 74:1; Jer 2; 31:9; Isa 11; 40:11; Zech 11:4-9).[57] Some unique features and motifs from the Old Testament are echoed in John 10: 1) The existence of both the good and false shepherd (Zech 11:4-9; Ezek 34); 2) The good shepherd is God's agent or God himself (Isa 40:11; Jer 31:9; Ps 74:1); 3) The folk refers to God's people—Israel (Ps 23; Isa 11; Jer 33); 4) The folk is threatened by the false shepherd (Jer 2; 10; 12; Zech 2); and 5) The sheep are saved by God through his messiah (Ezek 34; 37; Mic 5:3; Jer 32). The most interesting connection among all these is made between John 10 and Ezek 34; 37; and Zech 11:4-9. John 10:11, 14-15 and Ezek 34:23-24; 37:24-26 focus on the oneness and the identity of the true shepherd. The sine qua non for the gathering of the sheep into one is the one shepherd (μία ποίμνη, εἷς ποιμήν) (John 10:16; Ezek 34:23). In John, the shepherd refers to Jesus, where in Ezekiel it is to David.[58] Hence, it can be said that

---

55. Köstenberger argues that the language of "come in and go out" here "echoes covenant terminology, especially Deuteronomic blessings for obedience (cf. Deut. 28:6; Ps 121:8)." See Köstenberger, *John*, 304.

56. Deut 1:8, 11; 6:10-12; 29:12-13.

57. In the past, many scholars believed that the shepherd image in John was an allusion to Gnostic or Mandaean writings (cf. Bultmann, *John*; Appold, *The Oneness*). But, now scholars are aware that it is not the case. It is more likely that the image is derived from Jewish writings and the Old Testament respectively (cf. Dodd, *The Interpretation*, 98; Hoskyns, *The Fourth Gospel*; Schnackenburg, *St. John*, vol. 2; Brown, *John: 1-12*; Barrett, *John*; Carson, *John*; Hays, *Echoes of Scripture in the Gospels*, 319). It is interesting that even Bultmann agrees, contradicting his own view and theory, that the shepherd image in John 10 is derived from Ezek 34.

58. Pomykala has explored the connection between the Davidic Dynasty

The Shema and John 10

the allusion to Ezek 34; 37 in John 10 is meant to communicate the idea that David's role in gathering the scattered sheep is now fulfilled in the figure of Jesus (John 10:16; 11:52; cf. Ezek 34:11–24, 37:22–28).[59]

The underlying principle of this gathering is the covenant between God and the sheep (Ezek 34:25; 37:26; cf. Exod 3). The motif is echoed in John 10:14–15 in the use of the word γινώσκω. According to Keener, the word γινώσκω implies the covenant motif (see Exod 6:7; Jer 24:7; 31:33–34).[60] The passage of John 10:14–15 shows that Jesus knows (γινώσκω) and is known (γινώσκουσίν literally means the sheep know him) by his own in contrast to the false shepherd, who does not own or care for the sheep (cf. The false shepherd in Ezek 34).[61] This reciprocal knowing is based on (καθώς) the reciprocal knowing between Jesus and the Father (10:15).[62] The use of καθώς in this context, which underlines the foundation of the unity of the disciples as deriving from the unity of Jesus and the Father, is repeated in John 17:22 (also in John 14:10–11, 20).[63] In connection with John 10:28–29, this unity indicates the inviolable nature of the covenant, that is, the people cannot be snatched away because they belong to the one God—Jesus (John 10:28) and the Father (John 10:29).[64]

---

in connection with Messianism in his book, *The Davidic Dynasty Tradition*. In chapters 4–5 he argues that the figure of David is very prominent in Jewish Messianism. The Jews believe that one day God will send David-like figure to rule and unite His people. Cf. Ashton, *Understanding*, 255; Hays, *Echoes of Scripture in the Gospels*, 319–20

59. See Byers, *Ecclesiology and Theosis*, 99; Baron, "The Shema and the Gospel of John," 336–8

60. Keener, *John*, 817–8; cf. Köstenberger, *A Theology*, 459.

61. Another contrast is that the false shepherd oppresses and scatters the sheep (John 10:12–13; Ezek. 34:2–6), but the good shepherd gives his life and gathers the sheep into one (John 10:11, 14–17; cf. Ezek 34:11–16).

62. Forestell, *The Word*, 41, 120; Moloney, *John*, 304.

63. Murray, *John*, 302–3.

64. Barrett, *Essays*, 25; Hoskins, *Jesus as the Fulfilment*, 144; Hays, *Echoes of Scripture in the Gospels*, 319

The Shema and John 10 (2)

Another important point regarding the oneness of God's people is their identity. The fourth evangelist restresses the criterion used in the *Shema* in defining the people of God, that is, the relationship one has with God. As previously mentioned, in the *Shema*, the relationship with God is constituted through the covenant between him and his people.[65] This covenantal relationship is then the defining factor for the identity of the people of God. All rituals and religious practices are given to the people in order to "maintain" this covenantal relationship. To maintain means to always keep in mind the relationship they have with their God through this all rituals and practices.[66] However, what happens to the majority Jews of this period is that they make these rituals and practices, which are supposed to be used as a reminder of their relationship with their God, become criteria to define who the people of God are.[67] To the evangelist of the Fourth Gospel, the determining criterion to be the people of God is still the very criterion of the *Shema*—that is the relationship with God—as can be seen in John 10:16.

The statement of John 10:16 says "I have other sheep that do not belong to this fold." The phrase "other sheep" has been debated. Some scholars, like Martyn, suggest that the phrase refers to scattered Christian communities.[68] Some also argue that "the other" refers primarily to diaspora Jews.[69] Others insist that "the other" refers to Gentiles.[70] However, the context and background of John 10 do not support these suggestions. As mentioned earlier, the good shepherd image has been heavily influenced by the Old Testament, especially Ezek 34. Notably, both John 10 (John 10:12; 11:52) and Ezek 34 (especially Ezek 34:2–6) speak of the scattering

---

65. Wright, *The New Testament*, 260–2; Sanders, *Judaism*, 241.

66. Sanders, *Judaism*, 242–68.

67. As previously noted, Neusner has argued that the "true Israel" are defined by their relationship (knowing) with the God of Isarel. See Neusner, *Judaism When Christianity*, 91–3.

68. Martyn, *The Gospel of John*, 15; Howard-Brook, *Becoming Children*, 240.

69. Robinson, *Twelve*, 114–5.

70. Baron, "The *Shema* and the Gospel of John," 343–4

The Shema and John 10

and gathering theme (John 10:16; Ezek 34:13).[71] In its own context, the gathering in Ezek 34 may refer to "the uniting of Ephraim[72] and Judah under one shepherd (Ezek 37:22–24)."[73] It may then be argued that the evangelist in alluding to Ezekiel may be thinking about the gathering into one the Israelites and Samaritans.[74]

If this is the case, it is possible that "the other" in John 10:16 refers to Samaritans, since Samaritans are also mentioned in John 4. As stated in chapter 2, the Samaritans know, believe and practice the *Shema* on a daily basis.[75] The only thing that makes them different from the Jews is their ethnic (John 4:9) and cultic (John 4:20) identity. However, to those who belong to Jesus (including "the other" sheep), the worship place is no longer the issue, since it is already replaced by Jesus himself.[76] Both ritual (John 4:21) and race (John 4:39–42) are no longer applicable in speaking of having a relationship with God because he is revealed by the messiah he sent (John 4:25–26).[77] In this regard, "the other" in John 10.16 can, sociologically and theologically, be interpreted as the one who has a different social and ritual identity but has a relationship with God. Thus, the phrase "there will be one flock, one shepherd" should be understood as crossing both social and ritual boundaries.[78] It is significant that the *Shema* was always connected with the first commandant (the revelation of God's identity and saving act) in the Second Temple period (e.g., Nash Papyrus; 4QDeutn),[79] which implies that the relationship of the people of God have with

---

71. Byers, *Ecclesiology and Theosis*, 134–5

72. The reference to Ephraim in 11.54 indicates that Ephraim is no strange to the Fourth Evangelist.

73. Keener, *John Vol. 2*, 818.

74. Keener, *John Vol. 2*, 818; cf. Bowman, "Studies"; Freed, "Samaritan Influence"; Scobie, "Origins," 407.

75. Cf. van Der Horst, *Jews and Christians*, 134–5.

76. Neyrey, *The Gospel*, 118.

77. Hoskins, *Jesus as the Fulfilment*, 143–4.

78. It is safely presumed that this "crossing-boundaries" motif is also found in Paul's thought as clearly seen in his epistles to the Galatian and Romans. Cf. Yoder, "Introduction," 8–9.

79. Yoder, "Introduction," 3–4.

The Shema and John 10 (2)

the creator and saving God is based on God's revelation, neither on race nor ritual.[80] The obvious example of this case can be found in Josh. 2 and 6 which describe how the prostitute Rahab who is not a Jew counted to be the people of God. Josh 2 shows that Rahab has a knowledge and faith in the one God of Israel (and his saving act, Josh 2:9–11) and because of that she is willing to do what she does. As the result, as says Josh 6:25: "but Rahab the prostitute, with her family and all who belonged to her, Joshua spared. Her family has lived in Israel ever since," she and her family are counted and living as the people of God.

All this opens up the possibility that "the other" in John 10:16 may be extrapolated to include other groups.[81] In other words, "the other" may be better understood as whoever are willing to know and believe the God of the *Shema*. It corresponds with the use of ἐάν + τίς in John 10:9 which signifies the undelimited nature of the invitation to be the people of God. The only applicable category here is the relationship of human beings to God. This argument is supported by John 4:22 and John 11:52, where the gathering of God's people begins with the Jews, but not limited only to the Jews (as a nation, see John 11:52; Zech 2:11).[82] In addition, John 10:26–27 apparently gives a fuller picture to the puzzle, where the Jews are said as not belonging to Jesus' sheep because they do not

---

80. Neusner, *Judaism When Christianity*, 91–2.

81. Dodd, *The Interpretation*, 239.

82. Wahlde argues that John 10:16 and John 11:52 do not speak about the gathering of the people outside the Johannine community. The Old Testament passages alluded in both John 10:16 and John 11:52 do not refer to the gathering of the Gentile, he insists. But, he is not able to explain the phrase "not for the nation (ἔθνους) only, but to gather into one the dispersed (διεσκορπισμένα) children of God." In John's Gospel, ἔθνους is obviously refers to Israel (John 11:48, 50, 51, 52; 18:35), but, why does ἔθνους need to be connected with the dispersed children of God—and who are these children of God? In Ezekiel, the word "nation" rarely refers to Israel, but "the dispersed children of God" does. Moreover, in light of John 4:22, it is difficult to explain what the fourth evangelist means by "for salvation is from the Jews." Can it be understood as salvation is from the Jews to diaspora Jews? It seem to be unlikely. To make thing more complicated, it is also difficult to explain the reuniting of Ephraim and Judah in Ezek 37 if we exclude the Samaritans; cf. Davies, *Rhetoric*, 219; Klink, *The Sheep*, 202–3

The Shema and John 10

hear (ἀκούουσιν), know (γινώσκω), nor believe (πιστεύετε) in Him, in contrast to the sheep who hear, know and believe.[83] These verbs are inevitably very important to the Jews, especially in describing their relationship with God. In other words, these are meant to remind the Jews that the relationship between God and his people does not build on anything but on hearing, knowing and believing in God, which are crucial elements of the *Shema*. Therefore, it may be justifiably concluded that the identity of the one (gathered) people of God is defined by their relationship (believing and accepting) with the God of the *Shema*—who is revealed by Jesus the Shepherd who gathers them.[84] It includes not only diaspora Jews, Samaritans, Jewish Christians, but also all the Gentiles (see John 7:35; 12:20; 17:20; 20:29; Zech 2:11).[85]

In summary, John 10 uses two images from the Old Testament to explain the oneness of God's people. The first image is the image of the door. It is an allusion of Psalm 118. The door image functions: 1) To reveal the true Shepherd—the revelation motif; and 2) To identify the true sheep—the election and covenant motif. The second image is the good shepherd from Ezek 34 and 37. The allusion speaks of the foundation of the oneness of the people of God, which is the oneness of God (John 10:14–16). It also significantly clarifies the identity of the one people of God (John 10:16; 4:21–22; 11:51–52; cf. 7:35; 12:20; Ezek 34; 37).

---

83. Baron, "The *Shema* and the Gospel of John," 334–5

84. Cf. Pryor, *John*, 173–9.

85. Carson, *John*, 390; Brown, *John I-XII*, 396; Keener, *John Vol. 2*, 818–9; Köstenberger, *John*, 306–7; *A Theology*, 500–2; Schnackenburg, "Johannine Ecclesiology," 251; Lindars, *John*, 363; Dodd, *The Interpretation*, 239; Appold, *The Oneness*, 258; Moody, *John*, 208–9; Beasley-Murray, *John*, 171; Davies, *Rhetoric*, 201; Waetjen, *The Gospel*, 262–3, 265; Ridderbos, *The Gospel of John*, 362–3.

The Shema and John 10 (2)

The Eschatological Aspect: The Return of Yahweh to Zion.

As stated in chapter 2, Jewish monotheism is the mother of Jewish eschatology in the Second Temple period. The Jews believed and hoped that the One God of the universe would one day (through his Messiah) come and deliver his beleaguered people. And the dawn of this hope is the return of Yahweh to Zion, to his holy temple (Cf. Ezek 43.1–5; Isa 44–66; Hag 2).[86]

To the fourth evangelist, the eschatological expectation of the return of Yahweh to Zion has come to its fulfillment in the figure of Jesus. This can be seen, firstly, through the use of the setting of John 10 which is in the temple—the feast of the dedication (John10:22–23).[87] As repeatedly mentioned in the previous chapter, the temple (which is the symbol of oneness and Zion)[88] was already destroyed when the Gospel was being written. However, for the fourth evangelist the most important thing is not the restoration of the temple itself, but the coming of the one symbolized by the temple that, is Yahweh himself. This hope is fulfilled by the coming of Jesus as the replacement of the temple (see John 2:19–22).[89] This idea is strengthened by the allusion to the door image in Ps 118. Brunson argues that the door in John 10 may be related to the temple door of Ezek 10:18–9; 43:1–5.[90] Ezek 10:18–9 dramatically tell the departure of Yahweh from His temple and Jerusalem. However, Yahweh does not leave Zion without promising to return to reign over it again. The complete picture of this vision

---

86. Wright, *Paul and the Faithfulness*, 1049–50; Tan, *The Zion*, 23–51.

87. Brunson, *Psalm 118*, 335–6; Hoskins, *Jesus as the Fulfilment*, 173–5. Hoskins argues that John 10 concerns about the consecration of Jesus as the true temple [during the feast of the dedication] which is chosen to be the place for people to gather and worship God (p. 173).

88. Dunn, *The Partings*, 44–7; Davies, *The Land*, 50–4.

89. Brunson, *Psalm 118*, 338; Hoskins, *Jesus as the Fulfilment*, 104–46; Matson, "The Temple," 147–8; Davies, *The Land*, 289; Köstenbeger, *A Theology*, 422–30, 433; Dunn, *The Partings*, 124; Bauckham, *The Testimony*, 263–4; Moloney, *John*, 315–6.

90. Brunson, *Psalm 118*, 336.

The Shema and John 10

can be seen in Ezek 43:1–5, which speaks of the return of Yahweh to Zion, his temple.[91] Using this picture, the fourth evangelist wants to confirm that that eschatological hope is now fulfilled in Jesus—Yahweh has now come among his people through Jesus (John 10:7–10).

The return of Yahweh to Zion is also evident through the use of the good shepherd image in this chapter. Tan Kim Huat, in his survey of the Zion traditions, found that the "pastoral image was used to describe the action of Yahweh in the gathering of his people (to Zion) (Isa 40:11; Jer 23:3; 31:10; Ezek 34:10–16)."[92] Thus, it is clear now that the gathering of God's people has both ecclesiological and eschatological motifs (John 10:11, 14, 17–18; cf. John 11:51–52).[93] However, it should be noticed by now that the gathering image in John's Gospel, in which the ecclesiological and eschatological motifs are present, is not just a copy nor merely a continuation of the Old Testament and Second Temple hope. It has undergone development. The most difficult idea regarding the gathering of the people of God in John 10 is the medium for the gathering, that is the vicarious death of the Shepherd. According to Brown, this image is not explicit in the Old Testament (and Second Temple writings).[94] However, Köstenberger suggests that the concept may have been derived from Zech 13:7–9.[95] The problem with his suggestion is that the death of the Shepherd in Zech 13:7–9 does not result in the gathering of the sheep, but rather their scattering. It seems that the fourth evangelist is creatively combining the image of the shepherd and the sheep (lamb) in the vicarious death of Jesus (see John 1:29). If this is the case, it is plausible to argue that the image of the sacrificial lamb in Exod 12 and Isa 53 may be echoed here.[96] Both texts speak of the gathering and

---

91. Brunson, *Psalm 118*, 336.
92. Tan, *The Zion*, 29.
93. Thompson, *The Promise*, 84–5.
94. Brown, *John I-XII*, 398.
95. Köstenberger, *John*, 305.
96. Nielsen, "Old Testament Imagery," 78–80.

The Shema and John 10 (2)

deliverance of God's people.[97] More significant is the connection between vicarious death and love, the most important expression of the *Shema*, in John 10:17.[98] In the *Shema*, to love means to give up one's life to the one God.[99] Within this complexity, it seems that the fourth evangelist tries to make a connection between the love and deliverance elements in the *Shema* in order to explain the eschatological aspect of the gathering of God's people.

The deliverance element of the return of Yahweh to Zion can also be seen through the assertions like "I came (ἐγώ ἦλθον) that they may (ἵνα) have life (ζωὴν ἔχωσιν), and have it abundantly (περισσόν ἔχωσιν) (John 10:10)", "I (κἀγώ) give (δίδωμι) them eternal life, and they will never perish (μὴ ἀπόλωνται) (John 10:28)", and "will be saved (σωθήσεται), and will come in (εἰσελεύσεται) and go out (ἐξελεύσεται) and find pasture (νομὴν εὑρήσει) (John 10:9)."[100] The return of Yahweh is alluded to by the use of ἐγώ ἦλθον in John 10:10.[101] Yahweh does not come with no reason, He comes with a specific purpose (ἵνα) [102] that his sheep may have life (ζωὴν ἔχωσιν . . . περισσόν ἔχωσιν).[103] This corresponds with John 10:28 which says that Jesus (κἀγώ) [104] is now, in the present, giving (δίδωμι) eternal life (ζωὴν αἰώνιον; cf. Dan 12:2) to His sheep.[105]

---

97. Longenecker, *The Christology*, 48–50.

98. Baron, "The *Shema* and the Gospel of John," 355–7.

99. The most intriguing example is demonstrated by Rabbi Akiva when he recited the *Shema* before his death adding that this is the time to show his love with all heart, soul, and strength.

100. See Ezek. 34:14–15; Mlakuzhyil, *The Christocentric*, 316.

101. See Anderson, *The Christology*, 270.

102. I understand the use of ἵνα + subjunctive here functions as purpose-result clause. Thus, Jesus comes in order to give the sheep life, see Wallace, *Greek Grammar*, 473–4; cf. Dodd, *The Interpretation*, 144.

103. Baron has convincingly argues that the theme of life is closely related to the *Shema*, see Baron, "The *Shema* and the Gospel of John," 357–9

104. Usually used by Jesus to assure His sheep. See: Schnackenburg, *John*, 2.307; Köstenberger, *John*, 311.

105. W. Robert Cook remarks that "most of John's record of truth about eternal life relates it to the present." He is right, especially when we consider the eternal life as the result of the coming of Yahweh to Zion. It has to be in present. See Cook, "Eschatology," 88.

The Shema and John 10

This action of giving is followed by the assurance from the Father himself—that they will never perish (μὴ ἀπόλωνται), no one will snatch them out (of Jesus' hand in the future) (οὐχ ἁρπάσει) and no one has the power to do so (from the Father's hand in the present) (οὐδεὶς δύναται ἁρπάζειν).[106] The use of Jesus' and the Father's hand is once again an emphasis of their oneness.[107] In its wider context, we are told that the sheep have eternal life because the good shepherd has come to deliver them from the hand of the false shepherd (John 10:8, 10a, 12, 13). In order to deliver the sheep, the good shepherd must defeat the false ones as depicted in Ezek 34. This is obviously an echo of the return of Yahweh to Zion.[108] The people of God can be gathered into one (John 10:16) because the ones who scatters them (John 10:12) have been defeated by Yahweh. But there is a theological embellishment (of Ezek 34) here, depicted by the vicarious death of the Shepherd (John 10:15, 17–18). The defeat is not accomplished by anything but the sacrificial act performed by the Shepherd—in contrast to what the false shepherd does.[109] And again the idea of the sacrificial lamb in Exod 12 and Isa 53 appears and fits the context perfectly.

The onset of the return of Yahweh is to be differentiated from its consummation.[110] It is the start, rather than the end. The people of God have been gathered and granted eternal life, while the enemy is defeated. However, there is still final consummation to come.[111] This notion is interestingly shown through the use of some verbs which point to the future of God's people; The verbs

---

106. Thompson, *The Promise*, 34.
107. Loader, *The Christology*, 162; Barrett, *Essays*, 25.
108. Wright, *Jesus and the Victory*, 205–6; cf. Tan, *The Zion*, 29.
109. Cf. Ball, *'I Am'*, 94–7.
110. The same motif appears in 3:36; 5:24; 6:51; 11:23–27. Davies argues that, in those passages, the Gospel is revealing the concept of the present and future eschatology. Take 11:24 as an example where Jesus says, "I am the resurrection and life." The resurrection may refer to the present eschatology since the context of the narrative is the resurrection of Lazarus. The latter might refer to the future eschatology—that is the post mortem bodily life. See: Davies, *Rhetoric*, 160–1; cf. Robinson, *The Priority*, 340–1; Schenelle, *Theology*, 742–5.
111. Cf. Anderson, *The Christology*, 271; Forestell, *The Word*, 127, 129.

The Shema and John 10 (2)

are: will be saved (σωθήσεται), will come in (εἰσελεύσεται) and (will) go out (ἐξελεύσεται) and will find pasture (νομὴν εὑρήσει) (John 10:9).[112] Unlike the quality of life stated in John 10:10 and John 10:28–29, which is couched in the present tense, these verbs refer to the future state (expectation) of the people who (have) entered (εἰσέλθῃ) the community through Jesus.[113] Here we see how the fourth evangelist reworks his Jewish eschatology by adding the coming of Jesus into it.[114] To the Jews of the period, the return of Yahweh to Zion is the final act which will be followed by the vindication of the gathered people (cf. 4 Ezra 7:12–13; 8:53–54). To the evangelist, the return is the beginning of the drama. Scholars are right when they use the term "already but not yet" to describe this idea.

By way of summary, just as the Zion traditions are important for the Jews it is also important for John's Gospel. The fourth evangelist who is influenced by the *Shema* has incorporated the Zion traditions into the *Shema* with his eschatology. This is evident in the use of the two images, the door and the good shepherd, and some eschatological assertions. The door image echoes the leaving of Yahweh from his temple in Ezek 10:18–9. However, it is also at the same time a reminder of the return of Yahweh to his temple in Ezek 43:1–5. This promise, as seen by Ezekiel, is finally fulfilled in the coming of Jesus. The second image, the good shepherd, reminds the readers about the promise that the return of Yahweh will be characterized by the act of the gathering of his people. The echo of Ezek 34 in John 10:12 and John 10:16 shows that that

---

112. John 10:9 is on the one hand constructed in the form of conditional sentence (the use of ἐάν). So, the use of the future tense (σωθήσεται, εἰσελεύσεται, ἐξελεύσεται, and νομὴν εὑρήσει) can be seen as the apodosis of the protasis ἐάν τις εἰσέλθῃ. But on the other hand, as argued by Stanley E. Porter that the future tense can be more complicated than that. He argues that it is neither fully aspectual nor an attitude. For the survey, see Porter, *Verbal Aspect*, 403–27.

113. Again Porter argues that the Future Tense carries the expectation element (from subjunctive mood) in its usage. See: Porter, *Verbal Aspect*, 427, 438–9. This simply means that 10:9 can be understood as an expected event of all those who entered through the gate (Jesus).

114. Cf. Porter, *Verbal Aspect*, 403, 427–8.

The Shema and John 10

promise is also fulfilled by the coming of Jesus, since through his coming and death the people are gathered into one people under one shepherd. The nature of this fulfillment is further described by "the already but not yet" language in John 10. On the one hand, the people are gathered and living the eternal life given to them (John 10:10, 28–29). But on the other hand, there is still a greater consummation to come in the future (John 10:9). Thus, it is evident that the *Shema* has influenced not only the Gospel's theology and ecclesiology, but also its eschatology which is echoed in the Zion traditions.

Conclusion

Although the theological, ecclesiological and eschatological aspects of the *Shema* in John 10 are presented separately here, they are actually interrelated and inseparable. Each aspect connects and depends on the others. The theological aspect represents the uniqueness of Jewish monotheism—the *Shema*—along with the figure of Jesus. The fourth evangelist does not compromise strict Jewish monotheism, but rather (to use N. T. Wright's words) reworks it in the new category. Jesus and the Father are one (John 10:30), meaning that they belong to the same category, that is, the divine identity—so their oneness is the oneness of relationship. Through the context of John 10, we know that the oneness also falls into the category of revelational oneness, meaning Jesus reveals the Father through His works.

The ecclesiological aspect is essentially connected and dependent on the oneness of God—Jesus and the Father (John 10:14–16; cf. John 17). This fact is supported by the use of the image of the door and good shepherd in chapter 10. The door image, which is an allusion of Ps 118, functions as the boundary marker for the community of God's people. Those who belong to God's people have to enter through the gate—Jesus. The more vivid presentation of this aspect actually comes from the use of the shepherd image. This image is obviously an allusion to the shepherd in Ezek. 34. Both texts present the concept of the gathering of the sheep

The Shema and John 10 (2)

under one shepherd. This gathering is driven or motivated by the covenantal relationship between God and His people. The presentation does not stop there. It continues to introduce a new category for identifying the people of God. The people of God are no longer restricted by race or ritual, but by their relationship with the one God (Ezek 37:22-24; John 4; 11:52), meaning that the Gentiles are included as long as they have a relationship with the God of the *Shema* (cf. Zech 2:11).

The third aspect, eschatology, is also built on the other two aspects. The eschatology in John 10 is heavily influenced by the *Shema*—especially the Zion Traditions. In the Zion Traditions, the Jews believe that their God (theological aspect) will one day rescue and restore them (ecclesiological aspect) based on the covenant He has made. Once again, the relatedness of each aspect is shown by the use of the door and shepherd image in describing the eschatological aspect of the passage. The door image can be traced back not only to Ps 118, but also Ezek 10:18-9; 43:1-5. In these passages the door is depicted as the place where the glory of God leaves and returns the temple. The departure of God's glory had been experienced by the people of the period, but the return was awaited. In this regard, the coming of Jesus is seen as that fulfillment. The second image echoes once again the return of Yahweh to Zion, which is followed by the gathering His people (Ezek 34). The gathered people live now in the fulfillment age, but await the final consummation of the promised final restoration.

5

Conclusion

AS PREVIOUSLY STATED IN chapter 1, there are not many works that have been done on the subject of the oneness motif of the Gospel of John. As shown in chapter 2, the Gospel inherits the Second Temple Jewish understanding of the oneness of God which is deeply embedded in the *Shema*. Historically speaking, the Gospel of John, just as the Jews of the period (Jamnian Judaism) would, responded to the destruction of the Temple. This response focuses on the concept of the oneness of God and his people which is symbolized by the Temple itself. In other words, this response influences the oneness theme in the Gospel. Literarily speaking, the Gospel of John contains echoes and allusions to monotheistic or *Shema* passages in the Old Testament and other Jewish writings. Based on these findings, this book tries to understand John 10 both theologically and literarily using the *Shema* framework.

There are some obvious echoes of the *Shema* in John 10. These are in the form of the relational (covenantal) oneness motif (John 10:15, 16, 28, 30, 38; see also Deut 6:4; Num 15:41), the love motif (John 10:11, 15, 17–18; cf. Deut 6:5, 11, 13, 18), the deliverance motif (John 10:28; cf. Num 15:41; Deut 6:12; 11:3–7), and the hearing motif (John 10:3–5, 16, 27; cf. Deut 6:4). In addition, there are different aspects of the *Shema* that may be detected in John 10, which form the framework for this study (chapter 3); These are: the theological aspect (the oneness of God with the inclusion of Jesus in the oneness of God), the ecclesiological aspect (the oneness of God's people), and the eschatological aspect (the return of Yahweh to Zion). The theological aspect confirms that the oneness motif in the Gospel must be understood as relational and revelational. The relational oneness puts the relationship of Jesus and the Father in a new category, adapting to the divine identity (God) (John 10:30, 38), but without compromising Jewish monotheism. The revelational oneness explains the use of the subordinate language in John 10 in the way Jesus reveals the Father through his works.

Both the ecclesiological and eschatological aspects make use of the image of the door and the good shepherd, which are allusions to the Old Testament. Ecclesiologically speaking, the door image which is an allusion to Ps 118 functions as a boundary marker for the covenantal community. Those who belong to the community are those who know and are known by Jesus. This idea is supported by the next image, the shepherd image, which is an allusion (and an echo) to Ezek 34 and 37. John 10 speaks of the coming of the good shepherd, which is primarily to defeat the false shepherd and gather the sheep. Echoing Ezek 37, John 10 makes it clear, as it has always been with the *Shema*, that the identity of the sheep is to be defined by their relationship with the shepherd (covenantal relationship)—neither ritual nor race. The best examples of this concept are found in John 4 and 17. John 4 reaffirms that both race and ritual can no longer be used as a criterion in defining God's people. Similarly, John 17 states the oneness of God's people must be based on the relational oneness of Jesus and the Father. The key idea is the relationship between Jesus and the Father (cf. John 10:14–16; Zech 2:11).

Eschatologically speaking, the door image has something to do with Ezekiel's vision in Ezek 10 and 43. In Ezek 10, the prophet sees the glory of God leaving the people, while in Ezek 43 he sees the promised glory that will one day return through the same way and in the same place. The promise in Ezekiel's vision was deemed as yet to be fulfilled by the Jews of the Second Temple period. The

The Shema and John 10

fourth evangelist carefully uses this image with the Temple as the background, to show that Jesus is the fulfillment of this promise. The return of Yahweh is also depicted through the use of the good shepherd image. According to the Zion Traditions (rooted in the *Shema*), the Jews believed that Yahweh would one day return to Zion in order to gather His people under His reign. This hope never ceased during the Second Temple period. Using this image, the fourth evangelist tries to incorporate his "already but not yet" eschatology onto the Zion traditions he inherits. He construes the coming of Jesus as the return of Yahweh to Zion. This is marked by the gathering of the people and granting of eternal life to them. He also sees this return not as the consummation of the promise but the inauguration. In other words, the people of God live now in the end times, but await for the great consummation of God's promise.

This study does not claim to have resolved all issues relating to the positive influence of the *Shema* in the Fourth Gospel. There are still many aspects of the *Shema* that have yet to be fully explored in this book. But what has been discussed may arguably be very promising for further studies on the subject. To mention but three important topics that can be explored in studies to come. First, there are many other passages in the Fourth Gospel which relate to the *Shema* (e.g., John 4; 11; 17). The study of the *Shema* in John's Gospel can also be compared with the *Shema* in Paul and the Synoptic Gospels in order to understand the influence of the *Shema* on the early Church. Secondly, the political-religious setting (the Roman polytheist propaganda) of the Gospel[1] and its relation to the *Shema*[2] appears promising as a research topic. A study on this may shed light on the relation of the early Church and the politics of the time. Thirdly, a careful study of the use of the *Shema* in the Gospel of John, and other New Testament writings, can lead

---

1. See Richey, *Roman Imperial*. In this book, Richey argues that the Augustan ideology permeates to all layers of life in the first century. It also challenges the theology of the Fourth Gospel– particularly its Christology (chapter two of the book); cf. Salier, "Jesus, the Emperor," 284–301.

2. Otto, "Human Rights," Otto argues that the *Shema* can be seen as a reaction against Assyrian polytheist propaganda, where the Assyrian king is considered as a god.

Conclusion

to a mutual dialogue within monotheistic religions—Christianity, Judaism, and Islam (and Zoroastrianism). At the more technical level, a study can be done by comparing Christian, Jewish, and Muslim concepts of the oneness of God: שְׁמַע (the *Shema*) in both Christian and Jew thought and توحيد (the tawḥīd[3]) in Islam.[4] At the practical level, the *Shema* can be a good common ground for interreligious dialogue. Christians are often accused as being polytheist by the other monotheistic religions. This accusation can be clarified if Christians understand that their faith is monotheistic and deeply rooted in the *Shema*.

---

3. There are some different approaches to tackle this issue (of توحيد) in Islam's history, e.g. the strict monotheism by the Muʿtazilites, moderate approach by The Hanbalites, etc.

4. The oneness of God is arguably the heart of the dialogue between Christian and Islam as can be seen in the debate between ʿAmmār al-Baṣrī (the Nestorian) and the Muʿtazilah. However, the debate was focused on the philosophical category of the oneness of God (God's attributes: the knowledge and life of God). That is why the biblical understanding, especially the New Testament, will give another look for the dialogue. Cf. Griffith, "'Melkites', 'Jacobites,'" 9–55; Thomas, *Christian Doctrines*.

Bibliography

Anderson, Paul N. *The Christology of the Fourth Gospel: Its Unity and Disunity in the Light of John 6*. Harrisburg, PA: Trinity Press International, 1996.
Appold, Mark. *The Oneness Motif in the Fourth Gospel*. Tubingen: Mohr, 1976.
Ashton, John. *Understanding the Fourth Gospel*. Oxford: Clarendon, 1991.
Attridge, Harold W. "How Priestly is the 'High Priestly Prayer' of John 17?" *Catholic Biblical Quarterly* 75 (2013) 1-14.
Ball, David Mark. *'I Am' In John's Gospel: Literary Function, Background and Theological Implications*. Sheffield, UK: Sheffield Academic, 1996.
Baron, Lori Ann Robinson. "The *Shema* in John's Gospel Against its Backgrounds in Second Temple Judaism." PhD diss., Duke University, 2015.
Barrett, C. K. *Essays on John*. Philadelphia: Westminster Press, 1982.
―――. *The Gospel According to St. John*. London: SPCK, 1958.
―――. *The Gospel of John and Judaism*. Philadelphia: Fortress, 1970.
―――. "John and Judaism." In *Anti-Judaism and the Fourth Gospel*, edited by Reimund Bierringer et al., 231-46. Assen: Royal Van Gorcum, 2001.
Bauckham, Richard. "The Audience of the Fourth Gospel." In *Jesus in Johannine Tradition*, edited by Robert T. Fortna et al., 101-12. Louisville, KY: Westminster John Knox, 2001.
―――. "Biblical Theology and the Problem of Monotheism." In *Out of Egypt: Biblical Theology and Biblical Interpretation*, edited by Mary Healy et al., 187-232. Grand Rapids, MI: Zondervan, 2004.
―――. *The Climax of Prophecy*. London: T & T Clark, 2003.
―――. *God Crucified: Monotheism and Christology in the New Testament*. Grand Rapids, MI: Eerdmans, 1998.
―――. *The Gospels for All Christians: Rethinking the Gospel Audiences*. Grand Rapids, MI: Eerdmans, 1998.
―――. *Jesus and the Eyewitnesses*. Grand Rapids, MI: Eerdmans, 2006.
―――. *Jesus and the God of Israel*. Grand Rapids, MI: Eerdmans, 2008.
―――. "Messianism According to the Gospel of John." In *Challenging Perspectives on the Gospel of John*, edited by John Lierman, 34-68. Tübingen: Mohr Siebeck, 2006.

Bibliography

———. "Monotheism and Christology in the Gospel of John." In *Contours of Christology in the New Testament*, edited by Richard N. Longenecker, 148–68. Grand Rapids, MI: Eerdmans, 2005.

———. "The 'Most High' God and the Nature of Early Jewish Monotheism." In *Israel's God and Rebecca's Children: Essays in Honor of Larry W. Hurtado and Aland F. Segal*, edited by David B. Capes et al., 39–54. Waco, TX: Baylor University Press, 2007.

———. *The Testimony of the Beloved Disciple: Narrative, History, and Theology in the Gospel of John*. Grand Rapids, MI: Baker Academic, 2007.

Beasley-Murray, George R. *John*. Word Biblical Commentary 36. Nashville: Thomas Nelson, 1999.

Bennema, Cornelis. *The Power of Saving Wisdom: An Investigation of Spirit and Wisdom in Relation to the Soteriology of the Fourth Gospel*. Tübingen: Mohr Siebeck, 2002.

Bernard, J. H. *St. John Vol. 2*. The International Critical Commentary 32. Edinburgh: T & T Clark, 1928.

Boice, James Montgomery. *Witness and Revelation in the Gospel of John*. Exeter: Paternoster, 1970.

Borgen, Peder. "God's Agent in the Fourth Gospel." In *The Interpretation of John*, edited by John Ashton, 83–96. Philadelphia: Fortress, 1986.

———. *The Gospel of John: More Light from Philo, Paul and Archaeology: The Scriptures, Tradition, Exposition, Settings, Meaning*. Leiden: Brill, 2014.

Bowman, John. *The Samaritan Problem*. Pittsburg: Pickwick, 1975.

Brown, Raymond E. *The Gospel according to John: Introduction, Translation, and Notes, Vol. 1*. Anchor Bible Series 29. Garden City NY: Doubleday, 1966.

———. *The Gospel according to John: Introduction, Translation, and Notes, Vol. 2*. Anchor Bible Series 29. Garden City, NY: Doubleday, 1970.

Brown, Schuyler. "From Burney to Black: The Fourth Gospel and the Aramaic Question." *Catholic Biblical Quarterly* 26 (1964) 323–39.

Bruce, F. F. *New Testament History*. Melbourne: Thomas Nelson, 1969.

Brunson, Andrew C. *Psalm 118 in the Gospel of John: An Intertextual Study on the New Exodus Pattern in the Theology of John*. Tübingen: Mohr Siebeck, 2003.

Bultmann, Rudolf. *The Gospel of John: A Commentary*. Oxford: Basil Blackwell, 1971.

———. *Theology of the New Testament Vol. 2*. London: SCM, 1955.

Burkett, Delbert. *The Son of the Man in the Gospel of John*. Sheffield, UK: Sheffield Academic, 1991.

Byers, Andrew J. *Ecclesiology and Theosis in the Gospel of John*. Cambridge, UK: Cambridge University Press, 2017.

Carmichael, Calum M. *The Story of Creation: its Origin and its Interpretation in Philo and the Fourth Gospel*. Ithaca: Cornell University Press, 1996.

Carson, D. A. *The Gospel According to John*. Grand Rapids, MI: Eerdmans, 1991.

Charlesworth, James. *John and the Dead Sea Scrolls*. New York: Cross Road, 1990.

Bibliography

Chennattu, Rekha M. *Johannine Discipleship as a Covenant Relationship*. Peabody, MA: Hendrickson, 2006.

Coloe, Mary L. *God Dwells with Us: Temple Symbolism in the Fourth Gospel*. Collegeville, MN: Liturgical, 2001.

Coloe, Mary L., and Tom Thatcher. *John, Qumran, and the Dead Sea Scrolls: Sixty Years of Discovery and Debate*. Atlanta: Society of Biblical Literature, 2011.

Colwell, E. C. *The Greek of the Fourth Gospel*. Chicago: Chicago University Press, 1931.

Cook, W. Robert. "Eschatology in John's Gospel." *Criswell Theological Review* 3 (1988) 79–99.

Cowan, Christopher. "The Father and Son in the Fourth Gospel: Johannine Subordination Revisited." *Journal of the Evangelical Theological Society* 49 (2006) 115–35.

Culpepper, R. Allan. "The Pivot of John's Prologue." *New Testament Studies* 27 (1980) 1–31.

Danker, Frederick William. *A Greek-English Lexicon of the New Testament and Other Early Christian Literature 3rd edition*. Chicago: University of Chicago Press, 2001.

Davies, Margaret. *Rhetoric and Reference on the Fourth Gospel*. Sheffield, UK: JSOT, 1992.

Davies, W. D. *The Gospel and the Land*. Berkeley: University of California Press, 1974.

———. "In Memoriam: Charles Harold Dodd, 1884–1973." *New Testament Studies* 20 (1974) i–v.

———. "Reflections on Aspects of the Jewish Background of the Gospel of John." In *Exploring the Gospel of John: In Honor of D. Moody Smith*, edited by Alan Culpepper et al., 43–64. Louisville, KY: Westminster John Knox, 1996.

de Jonge, Marinus. *Christology in Context: the Earliest Christian Response to Jesus*. Philadelphia: Westminster, 1988.

Dodd, C. H. *The Interpretation of the Fourth Gospel*. Cambridge, UK: Cambridge University Press, 1958.

Dunn, James D. G. *Did the First Christians Worship Jesus? The New Testament Evidence*. London: SPCK, 2010.

———. *Jesus Remembered: Christianity in the Making vol. 1*. Grand Rapids, MI: Eerdmans, 2003.

———. *The Partings of the Ways: between Christianity and Judaism and Their Significance for the Character of Christianity*. London: SCM, 2006.

Ensor, Peter W. *Jesus and His Works*. Tübingen: Mohr Siebeck, 1996.

Ferreira, Johan. *Johannine Ecclesiology*. Sheffield: Sheffield Academy Press, 1998.

Flusser, David. *Judaism of the Second Temple Period Vol. 1*. Grand Rapids, MI: Eerdmans, 2007.

Bibliography

———. *Judaism of the Second Temple Period Vol. 2*. Grand Rapids, MI: Eerdmans, 2009.

Foresten, J. Terence. *The Word of the Cross*. Rome: Biblical Institute, 1974.

Frey, Jörg. "Love-Relations in the Fourth Gospel: Establishing a Semantic Network." In *Repetitions and Variations in the Fourth Gospel*, edited by G. Van Belle et al., 171-98. Leuven: Peeters, 2009.

Gerhardsson, Birger. *The Shema in the New Testament*. Lund: Novapress, 1996.

Goldenberg, Robert. "The Destruction of the Jerusalem Temple: Its Meaning and Its Consequences." In *The Cambridge History of Judaism Vol. 4*, edited by Steven Katz, 191-205. Cambridge, UK: Cambridge University Press, 2006.

Goodman, Martin. "The Temple in First-Century CE Judaism." In *Temple and Worship in Biblical Israel*, edited by John Day, 459-65. Edinburgh: T & T Clark, 2007.

Griffith, S. "'Melkites', 'Jacobites' and the Christological Controversies in Arabic in Third/Ninth Century Syria." In *Syrian Christians under Islam, the First Thousand Years*, edited by D. Thomas, 9-55. Leiden: Brill, 2001.

Haenchen, Ernst. *John 2: A Critical and Historical Commentary*. Hermenia 2. Philadelphia: Fortress, 1984.

Hägerland, Tobias. "John's Gospel: A Two-Level Drama?" *Journal for the Study of the New Testament* 25 (2003) 309-22.

Hanson, Anthony Tyrrell. *The Prophetic Gospel: A Study of John and the Old Testament*. Edinburgh: T & T Clark, 1991.

Harris, Elizabeth. *Prologue and Gospel: The Theology of the Fourth Gospel*. Sheffield, UK: Sheffield Academic, 1994.

Hays, Richard. *Echoes of Scripture in the Gospels*. Waco, TX: Baylor University Press, 2017.

———. *Echoes of Scripture in the Letters of Paul*. New Haven, London: Yale University Press, 1993.

———. *Reading Backwards. Figural Christology and the Fourfold Gospel Witness*. Waco, TX: Baylor University Press, 2014.

Herford, R. T. *Judaism in the New Testament Period*. London: Lindsey 1928.

Hill, Charles E. *The Johannine Corpus in the Early Church*. Oxford: Oxford University Press, 2004.

Hjelm, Ingrid. *The Samaritans and Early Judaism: A Literary Analysis*. Sheffield, UK: Sheffield Academic Press, 2000.

Horbury, William. *Jewish Messianism and the Cult of Christ*. London: SCM, 1998.

Horsley, Richard A. "'Messianic' Figures and Movements in First Century Palestine." In *the Messiah: Developments in Earliest Judaism and Christianity*, edited by James H. Charlesworth, 276-95. Minneapolis: Fortress, 1992.

Hoskins, Paul M. *Jesus as the Fulfilment of the Temple in the Gospel of John*. Milton Keynes, UK: Paternoster, 2006.

Hoskyns, Edwyn Clement. *The Fourth Gospel*. London: Faber and Faber 1957.

Bibliography

Howard-Brook, Wes. *Becoming Children of God: John's Gospel and Radical Discipleship.* New York: Orbis, 1994.

Howell, Don N. "God-Christ Interchange in Paul: Impressive Testimony to Deity of Jesus." *Journal of the Evangelical Theological Society* 36 (1993) 468–70.

Hurtado, Larry W. "First-Century Jewish Monotheism." *Journal for the Study of the New Testament* 71 (1998) 3–26.

———. *How on Earth Did Jesus Become a God?* Grand Rapids, MI: Eerdmans, 2005.

———. *Lord Jesus Christ: Devotion to Jesus in Earliest Christianity.* Grand Rapids, MI: Eerdmans, 2003.

———. *One God, One Lord: Early Christian Devotion and Ancient Jewish Monotheism.* London: SCM, 1988.

———. "Pre-70 CE Jewish Opposition to Christ-Devotion." *Journal of Theological Studies* 50 (1999) 35–58.

Josephus. *The Complete Works of Josephus.* Translated by William Whiston. Grand Rapids, MI: Kregel, 1970.

Kanagaraj, Jey J., and Ian S. Kemp. *The Gospel According to John.* Asia Bible Commentary Series. Singapore: Asia Theological Association, 2002.

Katz, Steven T. "The Rabbinic Response to Christianity," in *The Cambridge History of Judaism Vol. IV: The Late Roman-Rabbinic Period*, edited by Steven T. Katz, 259–99. Cambridge, UK: Cambridge University Press, 2006.

Keener, Craig S. *The Gospel of John: A Commentary, Vol. 1.* Peabody, MA: Hendrickson, 2003.

———. *The Gospel of John: A Commentary, Vol. 2.* Peabody, MA: Hendrickson, 2003.

Kittel, Gerhard, ed. *Theological Dictionary of the New Testament.* Grand Rapids, MI: Eerdmans, 2006.

Klink, Edward W., III. *The Sheep of the Fold: The Audience and Origin of the Gospel of John.* Cambridge, UK: Cambridge University Press, 2010.

Köstenberger, Andreas J. "Destruction of the Temple and the Composition of the Fourth Gospel," in *Challenging Perspectives on the Gospel of John*, edited by John Lierman, 69–108. Tübingen: Mohr Siebeck, 2006.

———. *John.* Baker Exegetical Commentary on the New Testament. Grand Rapids, MI: Baker Academic, 2007.

———. *A Theology of John's Gospel and Letters.* Grand Rapids, MI: Zondervan, 2009.

Köstenberger, Andreas J., and Scott R. Swain. *Father, Son and Spirit: The Trinity and John's Gospel.* Downer's Grove, IL: InterVarsity, 2008.

Lewis, Jack P. "The Semitic Background of the Gospel of John." In *Johannine Studies: Essays in Honor of Frank Pack*, edited by James E. Priest, 97–110. Malibu, CA: Pepperdine University Press, 1989.

Lindars, Barnabas. *The Gospel of John.* London: Oliphants, 1972.

Loader, William. *The Christology of the Fourth Gospel.* Berlin: Peter Lang, 1992.

Bibliography

Longenecker, Richard N. *The Christology of Early Jewish Christianity*. Studies in Biblical Theology 17. London: SCM, 1970.

MacDonald, John. *The Theology of the Samaritans*. London: SCM, 1964.

Mach, Michael. "Conservative Revolution? the Intolerant Innovations of Qumran." In *Tolerance and Intolerance in Early Judaism and Christianity*, edited by Graham N. Stanton et al., 61–79. Cambridge, UK: Cambridge University Press, 1998.

Martinez, Florentino Garcia. *The Dead Sea Scrolls Translated: The Qumran Texts in English*. Grand Rapids, MI: Eerdmans, 1996.

Martyn, J. Louis. *The Gospel of John in Christian History: Essays for Interpreters*. Eugene, OR: Wipf & Stock, 2004.

———. *History and Theology in the Fourth Gospel, 3rd Edition*. Louisville, KY: Westminster John Knox, 2003.

Matson, Mark A. "The Temple Incident: An Integral Element in the Fourth Gospel's Narrative." In *Jesus in Johannine Tradition*, edited by Robert T. Fortna and Tom Thatcher, 145–55. Louisville, KY: Westminster John Knox, 2001.

McGrath, James F. *John's Apologetic Christology: Legitimation and Development in Johannine Christology*. Cambridge, UK: Cambridge University Press, 2001.

McWhirter, Jocelyn. *The Bridegroom Messiah and the People of God: Marriage in the Fourth Gospel*. Cambridge, UK: Cambridge University Press, 2006.

Menken, Maarten J.J. *Old Testament Quotations in the Fourth Gospel Studies in Textual Form*. Kampen: Kok Pharos, 1996.

Michaels, J. Ramsley. *The Gospel of John*. The New International Commentary on the New Testament. Grand Rapids, MI: Eerdmans, 2010.

Mlakuzhyil, George. *The Christocentric Literary Structure of the Fourth Gospel*. Analecta Biblica 117. Rome: Editrice Pontificio Istituto Biblico, 1987.

Moloney, Francis J. *Sacra Pagina: The Gospel of John*. Collegeville, MN: Liturgical, 1998.

Moore, Anne. "The Search for the Common Judaic Understanding of God's Kingship." In *Common Judaism: Explorations in Second Temple Judaism*, edited by Wayne O. McCready et al., 131–45. Minneapolis: Fortress, 2011.

Moore, George Foot. *Judaism in the First Centuries of the Christian Era, Vol. 1*. Cambridge, MI: Harvard University Press, 1958.

Morris, Leon. *The Gospel according to John*. The New International Commentary on the New Testament. Grand Rapids, MI: Eerdmans, 1995.

Moyise, Steve. "Intertextuality and the Study of the Old Testament in the New." In *The Old Testament in the New Testament: Essays in Honour of J. L. North*, edited by Steve Moyise, 14–41. Sheffield, UK: Sheffield Academic Press, 2000.

Neusner, Jacob. *Judaism in the Beginning of Christianity*. Philadephia: Fortress, 1984.

———. *Judaism: The Evidence of the Mishnah*. Chicago: University of Chicago Press, 1981.

Bibliography

———. *Judaisms and their Messiahs at the Turn of the Christian Era*. Cambridge, UK: Cambridge University Press, 1987.

———. *Judaism When Christianity Began: A Survey of Belief and Practice*. Louisville, KY: Westminster John Knox, 2002.

———. *Messiah in Context: Israel's History and Destiny in Formative Judaism*. Philadelphia: Fortress, 1984.

———. "The Pharisaic Agenda: Laws Attributed in the Mishnah and the Tosefta to Pre-70 Pharisees." In *In Quest of the Historical Pharisees*, edited by Jacob Neusner et al., 313–28. Waco, TX: Baylor University Press, 2007.

Neyrey, Jerome H. *The Gospel of John in Rhetorical Perspective*. Grand Rapids, MI: Eedrmans, 2009.

Nielsen, Kirsten. "Old Testament Imagery in John." In *New Readings in John: Literary and Theological Perspectives*, edited by Johannes Nissen et al., 66–82. Journal for the Study of the New Testament: Supplement Series 182. Sheffield, UK: Sheffield Academic Press, 1999.

Olsson, Birger. "Deus Semper Maior? On God in the Johannine Writings." In *New Readings in John: Literary and Theological Perspectives*, edited by Johannes Nissen et al., 143–71. Journal for the Study of the New Testament: Supplement Series 182. Sheffield, UK: Sheffield Academic Press, 1999.

Otto, Eckart. "Human Rights: The Influence of the Hebrew Bible." *Journal of Northwest Semitic Languages* 25 (1999) 1–20.

Philo. *The Works of Philo: Complete and Unabridged, New Updated Version*. Translated by C. D. Yonge. Grand Rapids, MI: Hendrickson, 1993.

Pollard, T. E. *Johannine Christology and the Early Church*. Cambridge, UK: Cambridge University Press, 1970.

Pomykala, Kenneth E. *The Davidic Dynasty Tradition in Early Judaism: Its History and Significance for Messianism*. Early Judaism and Its Literature 7. Atlanta: Scholars Press, 1995.

Porter, Stanley E. *Verbal Aspect in the Greek of the New Testament, with Reference to Tense and Mood*. New York: Peter Lang, 1993.

Pryor, John W. *John: Evangelist of the Covenant People*. Downers Grove, IL: InterVarsity Press, 1992.

Rae, Murray. "The Testimony of Works in the Christology of John's Gospel." In *The Gospel of John and Christian Theology*, edited by Richard Bauckham et al., 295–310. Grand Rapids, MI: Eerdmans, 2008.

Richey, Lance Byron. *Roman Imperial Ideology and the Gospel of John*. Washington: The Catholic Biblical Association of America, 2007.

Ridderbos, Herman. *The Gospel of John: A Theological Commentary*. Grand Rapids, MI: Eerdmans, 1991.

Robinson, A. T. *The Priority of John*. Oak Park, IL: Meyer Stone, 1985.

———. *Twelve New Testament Studies*. London: SCM, 1962.

Sadananda, Daniel Rathnakara. *The Johannine Exegesis of God: an Exploration into the Johannine Understanding of God*. Berlin: Walter de Gruyter, 2004.

Bibliography

Salier, Bill. "Jesus, the Emperor, and the Gospel According to John." In *Challenging Perspectives on the Gospel of John*, edited by John Lierman, 284–301. Tübingen: Mohr Siebeck, 2006.

Sanders, E. P. *Judaism: Practice and Belief 66 BCE–66 CE*. London: SCM, 1992.

Schnackenburg, Rudolf. *The Gospel According to St. John, Vol. 1*. New York: Crossroad, 1990.

———. *The Gospel According to St. John, Vol. 2*. New York: Crossroad, 1990.

———. "Is there a Johannine Ecclesiology?" In A Companion to John, edited by Michael J. Taylor, 247–56. New York: Alba House, 1977.

Schnelle, Udo. *Antidocetic Christology in the Gospel of John: an Investigation of the Place of the Fourth Gospel in the Johannine School*. Minneapolis: Fortress, 1992.

———. *Theology of the New Testament*. Translated by M. Eugene Boring. Grand Rapids, MI: Baker Academic, 2009.

Scholtissek, Klaus. "Ich und der Vater, wir sind eins (Joh 10,30): Zum theologischen Potential und zur hermeneutischen Kompetenz der johanneischen Christologie." In *Theology and Christology in the Fourth Gospel*, edited by P. Maritz et al., 315–46. Leuven: Leuven University Press, 2005.

Schreiner, Thomas R. *New Testament Theology: Magnifying God in Christ*. Grand Rapids, MI: Baker Academic, 2008.

Schuchard, Bruce Gordon. *Scripture within Scripture: The Interrelationship of Form and Function in the Explicit Old Testament Citations in the Gospel of John*. Atlanta: Scholars, 1992.

Segal, A. F. *The Other Judaisms of Late Antiquity*. Brown Judaic Studies 127. Atlanta: Scholars, 1987.

———. *Two Powers in Heaven: Early Rabbinic Reports about Christianity and Gnosticism*. Studies in Judaism in Late Antiquity 25. Leiden: Brill, 2002.

Smith, D. Moody. "The Contribution of J. Louis Martyn to the Understanding of the Gospel of John." In *History and Theology in the Fourth Gospel*, by J. Louis Martyn and D. Moody Smith, 1–26. Louisville, KY: Westminster John Knox, 2003.

———. *John*. Abingdon New Testament Commentaries. Nashville: Abingdon, 1999.

———. "John." In *Early Christian Thoughts in its Jewish Context*, edited by John Barclay and John Sweet, 96–111. Cambridge, UK: Cambridge University Press, 1996.

Smith, Steven Charles. *Jewish Wisdom and the Gospel of John: Towards a More Critical Determination of its Influence*. Chicago: Umi, 2011.

Söding, Thomas. "Ich und der Vater sind eins: Die johanneische Christologie vor dem Anspruch des Hauptgebotes (Dtn 6,4f)." *Zeitschrift für die Neutestamentliche Wissenschaft* 93 (2002) 177–99.

Sohn, Seock-Tae. *The Divine Election of Israel*. Grand Rapids, MI: Eerdmans, 1991.

Bibliography

Spicq, Ceslas. *Theological Lexicon of the New Testament.* Translated and edited by James D. Ernest. Grand Rapids, MI: Hendrickson, 1993.

Stamps, Dennis L. "The Use of the Old Testament in the New Testament as a Rhetorical Device: A Methodological Proposal." In *Hearing the Old Testament in the New Testament*, edited by Stanley E. Porter, 9-37. Grand Rapids, MI: Eerdmans, 2006.

Stevick, Daniel B. *Jesus and His Own: A Commentary on John 13-17.* Grand Rapids, MI: Eerdmans, 2011.

Talmon, S. "The Concept of Māšîaḥ and Messianism in Early Judaism." In *The Messiah: Developments in Earliest Judaism and Christianity*, edited by James H. Charlesworth, 70-115. Minneapolis: Fortress, 1992.

Tan, Kim Huat. "Jesus and the Shema." In *Handbook for the Study of the Historical Jesus Vol. 3*, edited by Tom Holmén et al., 2677-707. Leiden: Brill, 2011.

———. "The Shema and the Early Christianity." *Tyndale Bulletin* 59 (2008) 181-206.

———. *The Zion Traditions and the Aims of Jesus.* Society for New Testament Studies 91. New York: Cambridge University Press, 1997.

Thettayil, Benny. *In Spirit and Truth: An Exegetical Study of John 4:19-26 and a Theological Investigation of the Replacement Theme in the Fourth Gospel.* Leuven: Peeters, 2007.

Thomas, David. *Christian Doctrines in Islamic Theology.* Leiden: Brill, 2008.

Thompson, Marianne Meye. "Every Picture Tells a Story: Imagery for God in the Gospel of John," in *Imagery in the Gospel of John*, edited by Jörg Frey et al., 259-78. Tübingen: Mohr Siebeck, 2006.

———. *The God of the Gospel of John.* Grand Rapids, MI: Eerdmans, 2001.

———. *The Promise of the Father: Jesus and God in the New Testament.* Louisville, KY: Westminster John Knox, 2000.

Tong, Far-Dung. "Gathering into One: A Study of the Oneness Motif in the Fourth Gospel with Special Reference to Johannine Soteriology." Ph.D diss., Christ Seminary, 1983.

Tukasi, Emmanuel O. *Determinism and Petitionary Prayer in John and the Dead Sea Scrolls: Ideological Reading of John and the Rule of the Community.* London: T & T Clark, 2008.

Turner, John D. "The History of Religious Background of John 10." In *The Shepherd Discourse of John 10 and its Context*, edited by Johannes Beutler and Robert Tomson Fortna, 33-52. Cambridge, UK: Cambridge University Press, 1991.

Urbach, Ephraim E. "Self-Isolation or Self-Affirmation in the First Three Centuries: Theory and Practice." In *Collected Writings in Jewish Studies*, edited by Robert Brody and Mosheh David Her, 229-63. Jerusalem: Hebrew University Magnes Press, 1999.

Van Der Horst, Peter W. *Jews and Christians in Their Graeco-Roman Context.* Tübingen: Mohr Siebeck, 2006.

Bibliography

Van der Watt, J. G. *Family of the King: Dynamics of Metaphor in the Gospel according to John*. Leiden: Brill, 2000.

Vanderkam, J. C. "Righteous One, Messiah, Chosen One, and Son of Man in 1 Enoch 37–71." In *The Messiah: Developments in Earliest Judaism and Christianity*, edited by James H. Charlesworth, 169–91. Minneapolis: Fortress, 1992.

Varghese, Johns. *The Imagery of Love in the Gospel of John*. Rome: Gregorian & Biblical, 2009.

Von Wahlde, Urban C. *The Gospel and Letters of John, Vol. 2*. Eerdmans Critical Commentary. Grand Rapids, MI: Eerdmans, 2010.

Waaler, Erik. *The Shema and the First Commandment in First Corinthians: An Intertextual Approach to Paul's Re-Reading of Deuteronomy*. Tübingen: Mohr Siebeck, 2008.

Waetjen, Herman C. *The Gospel of the Beloved Disciple*. London: T & T Clark, 2005.

Wallace, Daniel B. *Greek Grammar Beyond the Basics: An Exegetical Syntax of the New Testament with Scripture, Subject, and Greek Word Indexes*. Grand Rapids, MI: Zondervan, 1996.

Wright, N. T. *The Climax of the Covenant*. Edinburgh: T & T Clark, 1991.

———. *Jesus and the Victory of God*. Minneapolis: Fortress, 1996.

———. *The New Testament and the People of God*. Minneapolis: Fortress, 1992.

———. *Paul and the Faithfulness of God*. Minneapolis: Fortress, 2013.

Yoder, Perry B. "Introduction." In Take This Word to Heart: the Shema in Torah and Gospel, edited by Perry B. Yoder, 1–9. Elkhart: Institute of Mennonite Studies, 2005.

———. *Take This Word to Heart: the Shema in Torah and Gospel*. Elkhart, IN: Institute of Mennonite Studies, 2005.

Young, Frances. *Biblical Exegesis and the Formation of Christian Culture*. Cambridge, UK: Cambridge University Press, 1997.

Zimmermann, Ruben. "Jesus im Bild Gottes: Anspielungen auf das Alte Testament im Johannesevangelium am Beispiel der Hirtenbildfelder in Joh 10." In *Kontexte des Johannesevangeliums*, edited by Jörg Frey et al., 81–116. Tübingen: Mohr Siebeck, 2004.

www.ingramcontent.com/pod-product-compliance
Lightning Source LLC
Chambersburg PA
CBHW070511090426
42735CB00012B/2735